A Preliminary Look at Flourishing Congregations in Canada: What Church Leaders are Saying

flourishing
CONGREGATIONS INSTITUTE

AMBROSE UNIVERSITY

With Blog Collection Contributions by:

(in order of appearance)

Joel Thiessen, Bill McAlpine, Arch Wong, Keith Walker, Gordon T. Smith, Don Moore, Jeremy Duncan, Clara King, Joel S. Den Haan, Tim Beadle, Jerome Lavigne, Todd Petkau, Mark Buchanan, James Watson, Peter Coutts, Syd Hielema, Peter Schuurman, Sam Breakey, Milissa Ewing, Clint Mix, Cam Harder, Darryl McAuley, John Pentland, Lee Beach, April Yamasaki, Matthew Fillier, Timothy Quek, David Millard Haskell, Sam Reimer, Carla Leon, Jamie Holtom, Reginald W. Bibby, David Eagle, Kevin Flatt

Institute Website: http://flourishingcongregations.org/

A Preliminary Look at Flourishing Congregations in Canada: What Church Leaders are Saying

Edited by

Joel Thiessen, Arch Wong, Bill McAlpine & Keith Walker

flourishing
CONGREGATIONS INSTITUTE

Copyright © 2017 Flourishing Congregations Institute

All Rights Reserved

Published by

Turning Point
GLOBAL

Kingston, Saskatoon, Calgary, Kelowna, & Wellington, NZ

ISBN: 978-1-365-66105-1

Acknowledgements

Our research team appreciates the innovative and imaginative commitment that Ambrose University is making to launch the Flourishing Congregations Institute. We look forward to a strong partnership that benefits our students, colleagues, constituents, and the larger Church and Canadian society.

We are immensely thankful for the partners noted below, who took the first step to invest dollars in this Institute. We value their belief in empirical research as a helpful tool for church leaders across theological traditions and regions in Canada.

We express our gratitude to the 100+ leaders who participated in an interview and/or focus group, and to the many who have contributed blogs as a resource for others. Thank you for generously giving your time and expertise to this topic. We trust that your voices are captured in this monograph.

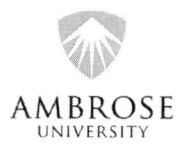

AMBROSE UNIVERSITY

World Vision
For Children. For Change. For Life.

WILLOW
The Leadership Centre Willow Creek Canada

UNIVERSITY OF SASKATCHEWAN

TRANSFORM
join the movement!

CANADIAN MIDWEST DISTRICT

Turning Point CONSULTING

CARDUS

Table of Contents

Acknowledgements v

Preface 2

Opening Remarks 5

Section I: Setting the Stage: Religious & Cultural Landscape in Canada 7

    Defining Flourishing Congregations 8

    Our Methods 11

    Institutional & Contextual Factors 13

    Faith Community in Exile 16

    Canada: Diverse, Inclusive & Tolerant 21

    Cooperation & Competition 26

    Immigration 31

    Few Churches Are Large 34

    Conclusion 36

Section II: Colleagues' Voices From
Across Canada: Blog Collection 37

Section III: Flourishing Congregations
in Canada: Preliminary Findings 169

    Introduction 170

    Early & Selective Findings 172

    Not Numbers . . . Or Is It? 173

    Clear Self Identity 177

    Vibrant Collective Spiritual Life 180

    Discipleship 183

    Leadership 186

    Outside the Box 194

    Hospitable Community 196

    Neighbourhood Presence & Involvement 199

    Evangelism 201

    Diversity 204

    Discussion & Conclusion 209

    Looking Forward 211

Section IV: Closing Engagement and Remarks 213

Closing Engagement: Dr. Sam Reimer 214

Closing Remarks: Dean Linda Schwartz 221

Closing Remarks: Dean Jo-Ann Badley 223

Editors' Postscript 225

Selected References 227

Preface

The Flourishing Congregations Institute officially launched with a public event on November 26, 2016, at Ambrose University, in Calgary, Alberta. This monograph captures the core content presented at the launch based in large part on a series of interviews and focus groups with Canadian church leaders in five Canadian regions in 2016. We also feature a series of blogs written by church leaders and academics across theological traditions and regions in Canada between early 2016 and early 2017.

Our aim with this piece is to begin a conversation. What exactly is a flourishing congregation? How should we define and measure this concept? What, if anything, is distinct about the Canadian context for thinking about congregational life, and moreover are there notable similarities or differences across Canadian regions? Where are the signs of congregational life and vitality across Canada? What can we learn – academically, practically, and theologically – from flourishing congregations in Canada? These are some of the questions that the reader may consider in reading onward.

As a research team we hold the contents of this document very lightly. We invite and welcome dialogue, push back, and suggestions. We anticipate that as our research unfolds, as we exchange ideas with others along the way, and as we receive constructive criticism, our collective understanding and analysis of Canadian congregational life will develop. To this end we share these preliminary set of ideas and observations.

But first, we want to provide a brief overview of the Flourishing

Congregations Institute. This is a research centre that is interdisciplinary and ecumenical in nature, embedded at Ambrose University and Seminary. The Institute brings together both academics and practitioners in collaborative ways to produce current scholarship and best practices related to congregations in Canada. Our long-term vision is to cultivate research analysis and application that accounts for theological and regional variation. That is, does flourishing look or feel the same in a Catholic setting versus a United Church of Canada context versus a Baptist environment? What about congregational life in Vancouver versus Winnipeg versus Toronto versus Montreal versus Halifax? It will take some time to make headway on these questions, but this is our intent in and through the Institute.

We do not naively assume that this Institute is the only or best place for serious research into Canadian congregations. We are aware of excellent research developing elsewhere and we envision the Institute possibly bringing these different academic, theological, and practitioner voices together for various events and publications.

Last, while we have an initial three-phase project laid out to begin our activities at the Institute, we foresee the Institute branching out into a series of specialized research projects in the short and long term – studies that hopefully foster careful and energetic research by many others across the country. For instance, we want to see more research devoted to rural congregations, ethnic and multiethnic congregations, church plants, mega-churches, and more. Though this first project will skim the surface of what can be known about flourishing congregations in Canada, the initiative will hopefully open the door to all kinds of possibilities that we believe other academics and church practitioners are interested in.

We invite you to connect with us at the Flourishing Congregations Institute.

Check out our website (www.flourishingcongregations.org), sign up for our email updates, follow us on twitter and like us on facebook, and join the conversation.

Joel Thiessen, April 2017

RESEARCH TEAM

Joel Thiessen, PhD
Sociology of Religion
(Principal Investigator)
Ambrose University

Arch Wong, PhD
Practical Theology & Religious Education
Ambrose University

Bill McAlpine, PhD
Practical Theology
Ambrose University

Keith Walker, PhD
Personal & Organizational Leadership
University of Saskatchewan

Opening Remarks for Launch of the Flourishing Congregations Institute

Gordon T. Smith, President (Ambrose University)

Welcome to Ambrose University. Ambrose sits on the traditional lands of the Blackfoot people and we are here by virtue of what is known as Treaty 7. We are Treaty 7 people and honoured to have this heritage. And we welcome to you our campus – especially if this is your first time here.

Delighted that you have joined us for this day to launch the Flourishing church institute. There are two observations I would like to offer as we launch the institution.

First, faith communities matter to us as a university. Many things matter us, but few more keenly and strategically than communities of faith – congregations. And we long for them to flourish. As a university, we long for the church to be all that it is called to be. At Ambrose, we often reference the language of Jeremiah 29, that we are called "to seek the peace of the city to which God has taken us." And we fully recognize that as a university we will only be able to fulfill this call – to seek the peace of the city – if and as we do it in partnership with faith communities. As a university it is for us a matter of theological conviction that the church is critical to the kingdom purposes of God.

Second, we recognize and affirm that the Institute is an interdisciplinary endeavour. As a smaller university we work to make this a point of particular strength. And it is so good to see this expressed in this project, that brings together pastoral theologians, leaders in the field of education, sociologists and others to think critically and clearly about the about the character of congregational life at such a time as this.

And it is our prayer that this institute would foster two things: first, good conversation, about what it means to be the church in our day; and, second, about those practices, that the institute would foster best practices that would equip the church to be precisely what it is called to be. And more, it is our desire that the institute – today and throughout the course of its work – would foster for you personally a deeper appreciation for the church and greater vocational clarity . . . for how you are called to be part of what God is doing in our world.

Let us pray.

God of Abraham and Sarah, the God and Father of our Lord Jesus Christ grant us this day this grace: to think clearly and courageously about the church and to foster the very best in congregational practice, witness and mission . . . for the well being of our country and for the sake of your kingdom. And encourage each one who has joined us today . . . may this be a day when they are encouraged and given greater vocational clarity. We ask this in the in the name of the risen and ascended Christ. Amen.

Section I

flourishing
CONGREGATIONS INSTITUTE

Setting the Stage: Religious and Cultural Landscape in Canada

A paper delivered by Dr. Joel Thiessen, on behalf of the research team at the Flourishing Congregations Institute Launch at Ambrose University

Calgary, Alberta, November 26, 2016

Setting the Stage: Religious and Cultural Landscape in Canada

AMBROSE UNIVERSITY

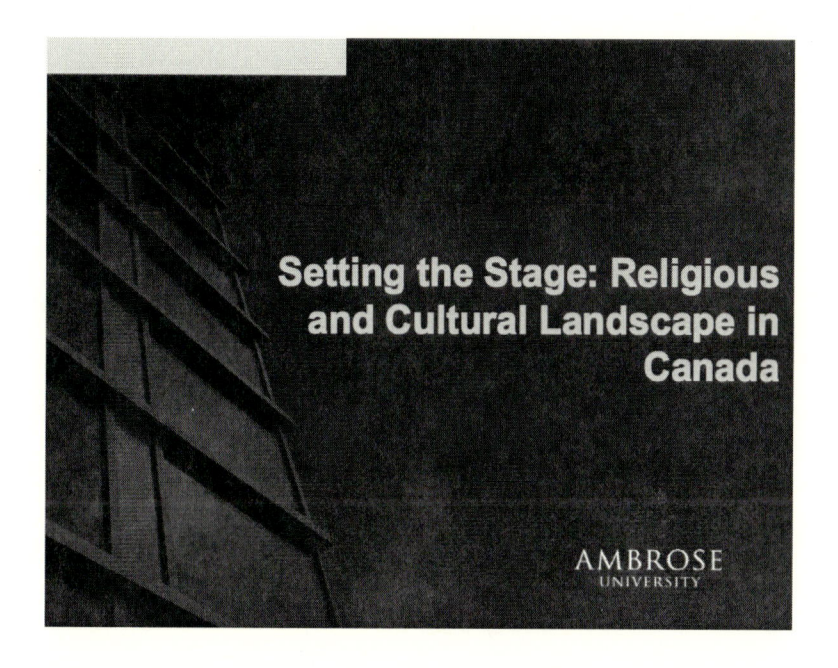

Defining a Flourishing Congregation ... A Start

As we launch this Institute we have not supposed or imposed a pre-set definition of "flourishing." Part of our purpose has been to inductively arrive at an expansive multidimensional understanding of how various Christian churches understand what a flourishing congregation looks like across Canadian social contexts and within their various theological traditions. Still, pragmatically we felt we needed to begin with a baseline of criteria from existing literature to enter this project. We were and continue to be keenly aware that our initial and stipulative or starting definitions will evolve, even dramatically, as our research progresses. We discerned seven initial attributes of flourishing congregations in the literature (see e.g., Ammerman 1997; Ammerman, Carroll, Dudley & McKinney 1998; Bickers 2005; Chaves & Anderson 2014; Dudley, Carroll &

Wind 1991; Dudley & Johnson 1993; Hoge & Roozen 1979; Hopewell 1987; Marti & Ganiel 2014; McGavran 1990; Roozen & Hadaway 1993; Scazzero 2010; Schwarz 1998; Wagner 1976; Wind & Lewis 1994; Woolever & Bruce 2004). We used these fairly well known and expressed attributes, indicators, or qualities as starting points for an emerging set of features in our research: a) quantitative growth in church attendance, membership, finances, and baptisms; b) active spiritual life among congregants: prayer, scripture reading, small groups, and volunteering; c) people are invited and welcomed into a vibrant sense of belonging and participation; d) worship services and mission are inspiring; e) leaders empower others to use their skills to lead and serve; f) faith-based outreach and service, within and beyond; and g) an active presence in the community at large.

Defining a Flourishing Congregation ... A Start

- **Active spiritual life** within congregations - prayer, scripture reading, small groups, volunteering, etc
- **Belonging** - people are invited and welcomed into a vibrant sense of community and participation
- **Inspiring Mission** - worship services and mission are inspiring
- **Quantitative growth** - church attendance, membership, finances, etc
- **Leadership** - leaders empower others to use their skills to lead and serve
- **Outreach and Service** - faith-based outreach and service, within and beyond
- **Community Presence** - an active presence in the community at large

Participating nominators and leaders self-declared that certain congregations brought to our attention met most or all of these criteria (see "Method" section below). In some cases they had other features in mind for "flourishing" that they felt ought to be included in the study. As we had anticipated, and as will become clear from our data analysis to date, our conception of flourishing has broadened and deepened based on how our interviewees described flourishing congregations. While we plan to parse out precise similarities and differences across Christian traditions for conceptualizing "flourishing congregation," it is too early in our data analysis and project overall to offer many substantive observations at this point. We expect this process of definitional and descriptive clarity to emerge as the research progresses. We also anticipate that this will provide us a more assuredly Canadian flavour to our understanding of and insight concerning flourishing in congregations. Furthermore, we anticipate that the concept "flourishing congregations" will be understood along a continuum of several indicators. What exactly those indicators and that continuum looks like is yet to be determined, as we move further into our analyses and engage in other phases of this program of research.

Our Methods for this Study

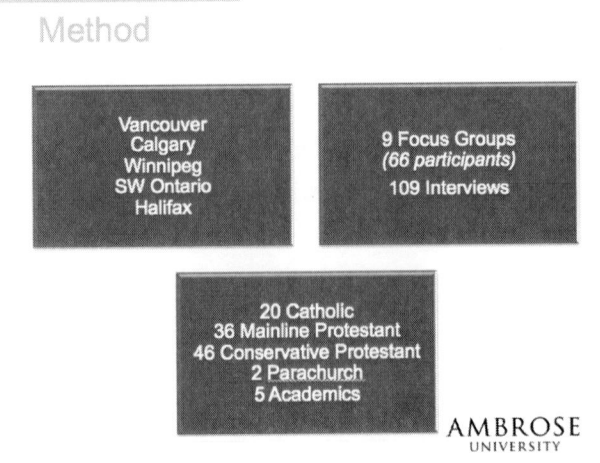

Method

Vancouver Calgary Winnipeg SW Ontario Halifax	9 Focus Groups *(66 participants)* 109 Interviews

20 Catholic
36 Mainline Protestant
46 Conservative Protestant
2 Parachurch
5 Academics

AMBROSE UNIVERSITY

Data collection took place between April and October 2016 in five Canadian regions: Vancouver, Calgary, Winnipeg, Southwest Ontario, and Halifax. In phase one of this study our sampling strategy involved approaching church and denominational leaders across Canada, asking them to refer us to flourishing congregations (as defined by them in concert with our preliminary set of descriptors described earlier). We reached out to nearly 400 individuals in this process. We then relied upon snowball sampling from those who agreed to participate, who put us in contact with other flourishing congregations. In phase one of this study we conducted nine focus groups with sixty-six individuals and we interviewed 109 church leaders. Many participated in a focus group and interview. Interviewees include twenty Catholic, thirty-six mainline Protestant, and forty-six conservative Protestant leaders. Despite our best efforts to increase the Catholic contingency in our sample, this remains a work in progress. We are gradually working our way through various gatekeepers, recently seeing our efforts yield additional interviews. We are optimistic that with more time we will successfully increase this group in our sample. We also interviewed two leaders in para-church organizations who regularly work with leaders of flourishing congregations, plus five academics whose research mainly focus on Christian congregations.

Taking an appreciative inquiry approach our focus groups centered on questions such as: When you hear the phrase "flourishing congregation" what comes to mind? Based on a series of themes discussed in the literature related to flourishing congregations (clear self-identity, committed leadership, desire to grow, hospitable community, and vibrant spiritual life), which of these themes stand out to you and what would you add to the list? Is there anything distinct or unique about the Canadian context (compared with the United States, western Europe, or the global south and east, for example), when thinking about flourishing congregations? Interviews went further to account for congregational history, critical turning points in the life of their congregation, descriptions of when their congregation is at its best, goals for their congregation over the next five years, and various pragmatic matters related to buildings and finances and partnerships.

In our two sessions this morning we want to share some of what we have learned to date. In this first session we will set the context by exploring how those in our study make sense of the distinct Canadian context for congregational life. In the second session we will offer some preliminary observations of how those we interviewed conceptualize what a flourishing congregation looks like (or ought to look like) in a Canadian context. To be clear we are at the preliminary stage in analyzing the data from interviews and focus groups. We are currently coding transcriptions and wanted to preview some of our initial findings through this presentation.

Institutional and Contextual Factors

Institutional/Contextual Factors

"Contextual factors are external to the church. They are in the community, the society, and the culture in which a church exists. A church has little control over them. Institutional factors are internal to the church and are aspects of its life and functioning over which it has some control" (Hoge and Roozen 1979: 39).

- Church as "gathered" and "scattered"
- Growing churches tend to stress internal factors; declining congregations tend to emphasize external variables.

AMBROSE UNIVERSITY

Social scientific research on congregations reveals that congregations are shaped both by institutional and contextual factors. According to Hoge and Roozen (1979: 39), "Contextual factors are external to the church. They are in the community, the society, and the culture in which a church exists. A church has little control over them. Institutional factors are internal to the church and are aspects of its life and functioning over which it has some control."

For example, contextual factors such as neighbourhood demographics (e.g., age, ethnicity, education, family status), the economic or political landscape, laws pertaining to religion, religious diversity, and the media can play an important role in growth, decline, or transformation of a congregation (Ammerman 1997; Ammerman, Carroll, Dudley & McKinney 1998; Dudley & Johnson 1993; Hopewell 1987; Parson & Leas 1993; Roozen 2011; Roozen & Hadaway 1993; Roxburgh 2011; Scheitle & Dougherty 2008; Wind & Lewis 1994; Woolever & Bruce 2008). So too can various institutional variables like leadership, programs, resources, processes and structures, theology, and a congregation's distinct culture, history, and identity (Ammerman 2005; Ammerman, Carroll, Dudley & McKinney 1998; Barna 1999; Bibby 1993, 2004, 2012; Bickers 2005; Bowen 2013; Bruce, Woolever, Wulff & Smith-Williams 2006; Carroll 2006; Chaves & Anderson 2014; Dudley, Carroll & Wind 1991; Dudley & Johnson 1993; Hopewell 1987; Iannaccone, Olson & Stark 1995; Kelley 1972; Macchia 1999; Marti & Ganiel 2014; McAlpine 2011; Reimer 2012; Roozen 1993, 2011; Roozen & Hadaway 1993; Scheitle & Finke 2008; Wilkes 2001a, 2001b; Wind & Lewis 1994; Woolever & Bruce 2004).

Another way to think about the institutional and contextual factors is theologically, using the image of the church as gathered and scattered. It is the church as gathered where they have control of what happens internally when it comes to the leadership, worship, and discipleship. The church as scattered is where we leave the doors of the church as God's baptized people to go into various contexts in the wider culture to bear the image of Christ, often times not able to control cultural variables to describe reality.

Research that explores church growth and decline suggests that church leaders and congregants in growing congregations tend to attribute their growth to internal factors that churches and its members have control over. Conversely, leaders and members of declining congregations are inclined to point toward external variables that they have little control over to explain their reality (McMullin 2013).

We focus our first session on the church as scattered, these contextual factors related to the religious and cultural landscape in Canada, which help to set up the overarching conversation about flourishing congregations in Canada. As we launch this Institute, a recurring refrain that we hear from many across the country is: "thank goodness this is a Canadian study on congregations." Though a heart-warming sentiment for our research team, the statement speaks to an underlying perception that there are distinct religious and cultural realities that set Canada apart from the United States, for instance, where most Canadian scholars and church leaders turn for congregational studies in the surprising absence of such research in Canada (only a few inter-denominational studies on congregations exist at all in Canada – see Bowen 2013; Reimer 2012; Reimer & Wilkinson 2015). As just one example, a denominational leader in a mainline tradition recently came to minister in Canada from the United States stated, "Of course stupidly when I first came here I thought 'well it's just about transferring the learning from one country to another.' Stupidly." Existing data reveals that Canada is far less religious than the United States; fewer participate in congregations, "religious nones" represent one-quarter of Canadian adults and one-third of teens, liberal values on most moral issues are the cultural norm, skepticism runs higher toward religious organizations, and most oppose mixing religion and politics. Moreover, Catholicism and Mainline Protestantism are the main expressions of Christianity, immigration keeps many churches afloat, and few mega-churches exist in Canada (see e.g., Bibby 2011; Noll 1992; Thiessen 2015).

How then do church leaders describe the Canadian religious and cultural landscape, and how do these descriptions compare with some of the empirical realities from the literature?

A Faith Community in Exile in a Secular Canada

When we asked interviewees to comment on congregational life in a distinctly Canadian context versus the United States, Europe, or Australia, one of the first observations to arise across traditions and regions pertained to how secular they think Canada is; fewer Canadians believing, behaving, or belonging to Christians groups, negative public images toward Christianity, and the marginalization of religion from the political realm.

A faith community in exile
- Declining levels of religiosity
- Christianity perceived as bad for society
- Canada between United States and Europe
- Religion in a private matter
- Religion and politics are separate

AMBROSE
UNIVERSITY

A conservative Protestant leader in southwestern Ontario lamented, "A significant number of Canadians don't feel guilty about not going to church." Others conveyed their perception that Canadians generally think religion, and Christianity in particular, is bad for society. Here we see two conservative Protestants exchange views in a focus group in Ontario:

> *[Respondent 1]* We talk sometimes about good news. I think for Canadians, they don't feel like Christianity, Jesus, the gospel, the cross – I don't think they feel like that's news ... And they don't think the church is good. The church is that institution that ripped kids out of their First Nations village, lured them onto float plane with candy and took them away from their family, and their family never saw them again. Or they went back to their community after suffering sexual abuse and brought that pain and damage back to their home community. It's the place where the priests have been pedophiles. So even though every profession has pedophiles, the church is in the media as being the one that somehow is sort of the icon of pedophilia. The church has earned a place in Canadian society where people are questioning its goodness.
>
> *[Respondent 2]* I can't say yes to that enough. That feels precisely, in my mind the task of communicating the Christian message is taking something that's familiar and trying to make it actually unfamiliar again. And because I agree, I don't think the issue is the story out there, it is – it's somehow reframing, repackaging in a way that sounds unfamiliar or is detached from what I think many people see in Canada as, maybe not an evil institution, but I don't

think people are neutral on the church. I think people have slightly indifferent, negative views of the church's past.

As interviewees made these claims they also consistently located Canada's religious past, present, and possible future somewhere between the United States and Europe. A United Church of Canada leader in the Maritimes noted, "We're not as secular as Europe or Britain but we're more secular than the U.S. So we have this – I refer to it as the HSM, the Holy Shit Moment – when a regional church knows post-Christendom has just arrived." Some that we spoke to shared how they turn to the United Kingdom for resources and insights, to anticipate where the Church in Canada may be headed. In one of our focus groups in Toronto a mainline Protestant leader indicated, "The U.K. is actually further along the curve when it comes to social enterprise in understanding social innovation … we're actually following the U.K. … we're about a decade behind." Later the same individual noted that some congregations in the United States are turning to their Canadian counterparts, "So we're like 'yes! The U.S. can learn from Canada, thank you very much.'" Members around the focus group proceeded to clap in response, affirming that Canada has something to offer the American Church rather than always the other way around.

One identified implication of a secular context is that religious belief and practice remains private, kept from the public realm. A mainline Protestant pastor in Calgary denoted, "I think in the States you can ask people what church they go to, you wouldn't do that in Canada; we're more private." A focus group participant in the Maritimes described his read of Canadians toward religion as, "A very private thing. It's not a public conversation. It's not

18

something I need to hear in dinner or when we're having coffee that you know which church I go to or what I think about those things. I hold those cards close to my chest." A Catholic leader in Calgary stated, "Canada is more passive and less outspoken." A conservative Protestant pastor in Ontario declared in a focus group, "I spent a year discipling some young adults who found it even difficult to even self-identify publicly as a Christian, in work situations, in social networks. So a whole lot of social pressure to keep that identity to themselves, let alone even talking about it."

Statements such as these frequently intersected with reflections about religion and politics, which the literature shows is one of the major differences between Canada and the United States (see e.g., Reimer 2003; Reimer & Wilkinson 2015). A United Church of Canada leader in Halifax reflected during a focus group discussion, "I can't get over how many times I hear somebody in church say religion and politics are two separate things … which is hilarious to think of the Gospel not being political." A Catholic leader in Halifax said during an interview that Canadians tend not to link Christianity with a specific political party; "I just found Americans to be very polarized. So when it comes to politics you're either right or left. You're either Republican or Democrat." Another leader in the Maritimes illustrated the Canadian distinctive well: "I can still remember the shock and gasps when Stephen Harper completed a speech with "God bless Canada" 'cause our politicians just don't do that normatively." In one of our focus groups in Ontario, the following exchange linked the media, politics in the United States, and Canadian perceptions toward evangelicals:

> *[Respondent 1]* Canadians are happy to not have religion in politics.

[Respondent 2] I think we reap the media overflow from the States.
[Respondent 1] Absolutely.
[Respondent 2] So that some American says, "well I believe God says we should go into this country and assassinate this person or some guy talks about 2 Corinthians on stage, who's apparently going to be in a very important position in the United States," and it seems like certain people in Canada say, "oh well that's Christians."
[Respondent 1] Absolutely.
[Respondent 2] Right. Those key sound bites provide a filter then for the non-churched Canadians to view the churched Canadians.
[Respondent 1] I would say that's one of my biggest battles, is understanding that people's view of Christian Evangelical is shaped not by Canada but by what we're hearing coming through the States.
[Respondent 3] With Republicans in the U.S.
[Respondent 1] Yeah and I mean that's a very trying to separate that is a bit of a missional task.
[Respondent 2] Yeah that's right. It is.

Reflective of the historical, cultural, religious, and political differences between Canada and the United States, an Anglican leader in Toronto spoke about a conservative oriented Episcopalian preacher visiting from the United States who "could not figure out how his congregation would consistently vote NDP. For him there was an identity between Republican values and evangelical Christianity."

In sum, participants in this study described Canada as a very secular society, distinguished from the United States most in terms of the separation between religion and politics. In many ways these reflections are strongly correlated with the next substantive topic to arise in our research to date: Canadian values for diversity, inclusivity, and tolerance.

Canada: A Diverse, Inclusive, and Tolerant Nation

Layered within a secular Canada is a belief among many of those we met that Canada is a very inclusive and tolerant society, where exclusivity and offending others is deemed "un-Canadian." At the same time there is a perception that Canadian rhetoric toward inclusivity is at times exclusivist towards Christianity in ways that leave Christians on the margins of Canadian social life. In many of the following examples it is interesting to note how frequently politics once more enters the discussion.

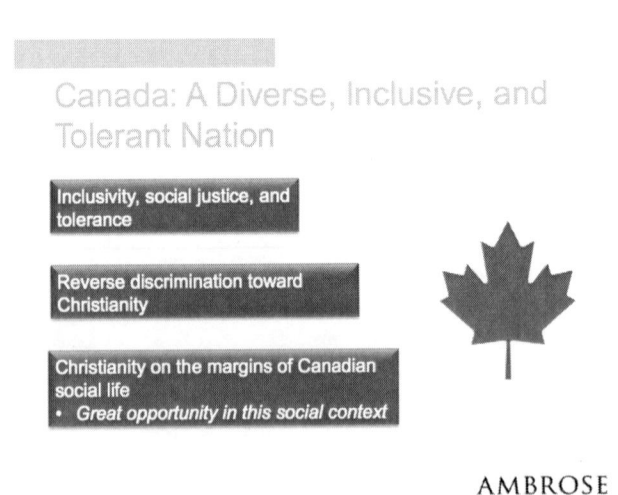

Canada: A Diverse, Inclusive, and Tolerant Nation

- Inclusivity, social justice, and tolerance
- Reverse discrimination toward Christianity
- Christianity on the margins of Canadian social life
  • Great opportunity in this social context

AMBROSE
UNIVERSITY

In one of our interviews with a Catholic leader in Vancouver, he observed, "I think we're very Canadian so we're not a very polarized group. This group would probably vote to stay in the E.U. and it probably wouldn't go for the extremes of a Trump sort of thing. They probably, if they got to vote for the president of the United States, they'd vote for Bernie Sanders. Yeah, so it feels very Canadian." Our data collection took place in Spring 2016 and we heard numerous references to Donald Trump and the aversion in Canada to vote for Trump due to Canada's value for diversity, inclusivity, and tolerance. A mainline Protestant denominational leader in Ontario who has ministry experience in both Canada and the United States provided a reflection on politics and tolerance across the borders:

> There [United States] the church is totally connected to the Republican Party, the word social justice is a swear word. Moving back here, I was really struck by how close Christian culture is, and how the spirit of tolerance. And I think the challenge for flourishing here is that tolerance is low accountability, but to be the church in a post-Christian context, kind of requires high accountability. And so you get this competing dynamics of accountability; which I can see a struggle with the congregation that I'm part of, and also in my own work. But I think it's a real blessing that the Canadian Church is not really connected to a political party in most of the country. That there's much more capacity for a hospitable community to evolve, to have a commitment to social justice, I think is a beautiful thing.

A Catholic leader in Ontario mentioned that a flourishing congregation in Canada is evaluated on its ability to discover "all of the fringes of what the teachings are and what can they – not so much get away with – but how can they be so inclusive of many other areas and levels … If I go to Detroit, the answer is black or white. If I come to Windsor across the road, well we live in the greys. And right across Niagara Falls and New York, it's the same, St. Catherine's. It's pretty much the same across Canada from my experience."

There is a sense among some interviewees that Canada's propensity to be inclusive and tolerant has contributed to a reverse discrimination of sorts toward Christianity. A leader of an ethnic congregation in Winnipeg recalled his early days in ministry in Canada:

> Actually one of my shocks here when I came and I was involved in the serving or welcoming the new citizens and, few years ago what I – citizenship they gave bibles to new Canadians. And so when I first offered that we welcome people I said, "Where are the bibles, because we are excited to give the bibles . . . Oh they are no longer allowing that because it is – don't want to offend other religions." I said, "Oh I thought I came to Canada a free country where I can express my [Faith]" – you are free to reject or accept whatever giving you but don't prevent me from doing what I think is just good. I mean I give you this literature if you don't to then I respect that. But don't stop me from distributing this free literature saying, "Oh I want to offend you." So that's really shocked me and I said, "No way we are in a free country I left the Philippines I thought that they are still have you know well we are free there but I thought Canada is really a free country why can I not – why am I restricted to do this?" And even you know don't distribute literatures in the malls because you don't

want to offend the people. I said, "No we are free country we thought that this."

This participant's account intersects with a broader narrative that we heard, of Christianity seemingly on the margins of Canadian social life. This new terrain is unfamiliar for some. A United Church of Canada minister in Halifax offered this reflection, "We're trying to learn what it means to be displaced to the margins but we don't have a lot of history of telling that story. And that really gets in the way 'cause we don't know who we are. We used to be part of the political establishment in running things. We're not there anymore but we don't have a tradition of storytelling, evangelism, and whatever you want to call it which makes it really hard." A denominational leader in the Anglican Church of Canada discussed the challenges that arise from the margins:

> We're not invited into the conversation discourse. For example, you know, the big topic of physician assisted death. If they think it's going to be controversial they're going to get someone to say something sensational. But to be part of that conversation … we're on the margins in terms of having a voice. And we have to fight our way into having a voice about issues that affect the people that we minister to and with … But we want to be involved in that conversation about who we are and what we hold and value and why, and how does that speak to us as a people of faith?

Others, like the following mainline Protestant leader, extended this sentiment further, suggesting that other religious traditions are given preferential treatment in society over and against Christians: "The larger society is actively casting us off, is actively moving us to the margins. For example, I think that it would be much more likely that a Shambhalic Buddhist would be invited to do something in the midst of a civic ritual or ceremony. Or, now, an Aboriginal person, a Mi'kmaq person, would be much, much more likely to give leadership in some kind of a civic ritual than a church leader."

Several respondents framed this Canadian context as a great opportunity to minister from the margins of Canadian social life. Some respondents made Biblical comparisons to Jesus and Christianity on the whole that, in their view, seemingly flourished from the margins rather than the center of social and cultural life. During one of our focus groups in Ontario a respondent encouraged all in the group to "look around at the church on the borderland versus the church at the centre … we have to figure out how it is we serve on the borderland which is historically where church has been the best. And I think those are all fairly unique Canadian opportunities." During a focus group in Calgary, a conservative Protestant leader signaled:

> I was down in the States for a couple of years not too long ago … to hear the cultural conversation there was interesting, hearing them feel like, "oh the church is going to go into exile because the country is becoming less Christian." And I was like, "dude, get over it, it's actually a good thing, it's fine" … bringing it back to Canada then …it feels that the assumption is that we're not in a Christian culture, we're in a post-Christian culture in a lot of ways. And that actually creates opportunity, once you start thinking of it that way, there's actually more space.

A respondent in a focus group in Winnipeg expressed his reflections on the opportunity of ministering from the margins, "For me it's the advantage of knowing you're in exile. I think most my family's American and they're dealing with kind of the falling of the empire and they're trying to hang on ... It's so much more difficult for them I think to actually have an integrated, growing, vibrant, spiritual life/faith. In a backdrop that's just so, grey and kind of loosely Christian but not really identifiably so. So I think it's a huge advantage."

Later we will see some of the specific ways that respondents link "living in exile" in a tolerant and diverse social context with their understanding of what it means to be a flourishing congregation in Canada in the 21st Century.

Cooperation versus Competition

Part of the Canadian ethos for inclusivity translates into the assertion among some leaders that Canadian congregations are far more cooperative and collaborative versus those in the United States. Such collaboration takes on multiple forms from partnering with other congregations within one's denomination, to collaborating with congregations in other Christian traditions, to coming together with other faith groups altogether, to partnering with various secular agencies toward a common cause that will benefit one's community.

Cooperation vs. Competition

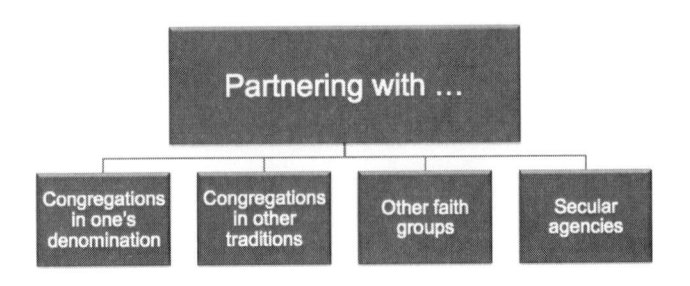

Partnering with ...

- Congregations in one's denomination
- Congregations in other traditions
- Other faith groups
- Secular agencies

AMBROSE
UNIVERSITY

One participant in a focus group in Ontario discussed the breaking down of denominational walls in Canada, "I am seeing or sensing the softening of denominational walls and maybe a willingness to relinquish them to do stuff together more ... I just think we're all kind of shifting in that direction a little more. Post-denominalization maybe. I doubt they're going to disappear, but partnerships across tribal lines have become very, very important. I know church planting, whether the AGC and the Christian Missionary Alliance and us, we get together and co-plant churches – people love that. Who cares who ends up getting that congregation or what the label is on the door after the fact. That seems to be hot right now." This topic arose in a focus group in Winnipeg as well, as participants reflected on the challenges or opportunities connected with being "in exile" in Canada: "I also think that there's a greater generosity between the Anglican, Catholic, and range of evangelical traditions in Canada than what I experienced in the US. There are far sharper lines dividing things, even within tribes. And there's the same dividing – we have to band together and appreciate each other for the simple stake of encouragement if nothing else."

From our data collection and analysis thus far it appears that pan-religious collaborations are more commonly found in United Church of Canada settings. Below is an exchange centered among a few participants in the United Church of Canada in one of our focus groups.

> *[Respondent 1]* Think about celebrations in December, we're going to get to a time where Halifax is comfortable celebrating Christmas and Diwali, Hanukah, and whatever month Ramadan happens in and Eid, we'll celebrate that. And that'll be a great moment 'cause it's both/and.
> *[Respondent 2]* It's getting there.
> *[Respondent 1]* Well the way to there has been none of the above, right? [agreement around the room] ... One of the things I've found really helpful and hopeful in this regard is the values and vision series that [ABC Church] and Shambhala in the Unitarian Church and sometimes a synagogue have done together. So we've had all candidates debates for a federal election, municipal election. We organized an event on doctor-assisted death and people showed because we weren't one faith or we weren't just Christians. And I think that that has been a way to re-enter, however humbly, the public sphere.
> *[Respondent 3]* This is kind of this interesting cultural moment for Canada in church as this sort of multi-cultural project continues, right? And we're watching those tensions bubble over and boil over in the States and in England in particular. But for us there's this interesting space now, because we've done that ground clearing, is whether the church and other faith leaders take it upon themselves to create more spaces for

conversation. So you're going to continue to diversify the population but one of the issues is that what happens when everybody retreats to their own enclave in their community, you don't know your neighbour. Why does your neighbour do those things? Who is your neighbour? Whereas the more we do work or we engage other faith communities to come together to talk and begin to break down the stereotypes that are often perpetrated on a very surface level in the media, the more you create opportunities for real capacity, community relationships to form and new things to happen and that'll be a huge gift to Canada instead of Canada turning into a light version of what we're seeing in the States along the attitudes around immigration and who's in and who's out.

[Respondent 1] It's been fascinating over the last two years. We cancel all the meetings during Lent and we have conversation with our faith neighbours and the basic premise of the conversation is help us to understand what it means to be you in Canada today. And I don't know what's more interesting: the response from other Christian leaders that are interested in having these conversations, or the response from the people from other faiths to say, "You're serious? You're really interested?" There is this sense of those impenetrable walls. And I think one of the roles that flourishing congregations might provide is that safe space where things of the spirit and things of religious practice can actually be talked about because we take them seriously. We don't necessarily do them in the same way but we take them seriously.

[Respondent 2] I guess the counter or the difficulty in some of that that I've certainly experienced in my community around even trying to engage other Christian communities in conversation is that some are so set in a particular theological framework that they won't engage with a woman who's in ministry. They won't engage with the United Church because they don't believe the United Church is actually Christian because of our belief system and our stance on things. And so that doesn't mean that we don't try to engage in that but it certainly makes it very difficult. And I think it strikes me that most often the media representation of the Christian church is narrow-minded, homophobic, judgmental, not particularly inclusive, and not particularly welcoming to people of other faiths. And so when that's the dominant image that's put forward, it's no wonder they don't want us to be invited to do anything because we're simply going to tell everybody else that they're wrong until they think like us. So that's been an experience.

The concluding reflections in this exchange suggest there is not a uniform openness or embrace toward inclusive cooperation. In later phases of our research we want to explore this and other related themes further. For example, do flourishing congregations embrace cooperation and collaboration as much as is suggested in phase one of this research? How is this narrative expressed in concrete terms? Are there indicators of competition in congregational life relative to other congregations within or across denominational or religious lines, and if so, how is such competition played out? How do congregants approach and experience cooperation and/or competition? These questions intersect with a longstanding theoretical argument in the sociology of religion, rational choice theory, that groups which exist in a competitive religious marketplace are positioned to thrive as they seek to sharpen their religious product and supply of religion (e.g.,

Stark & Finke 2000). We hope to test some of these claims out in the Canadian context.

Immigration

- Benefits Canadian congregations (especially Catholic and conservative Protestant)
- Foreign-born appear more conservative and countercultural

AMBROSE
UNIVERSITY

It is no secret that one of the hallmarks of Canadian social life is its openness to immigration and multiculturalism. As a Catholic leader in Vancouver stated, "Diversity, I think, is a very positive component of parish life because basically that really reflects what Canada is when you think about it." Later we will explore interviewee beliefs regarding the sociological and theological ties between diversity and flourishing congregations. For now we simply want to highlight a couple of the implications that immigration has for congregational life.

Most obviously, as immigration to Canada from the global south and east continues to rise – from places where the global epicenter of Christianity exists – Canadian congregations benefit, particularly in Catholic and some conservative Protestant settings (Bibby & Reid 2016). Sometimes immigration results in a series of mono-ethnic congregations. A Catholic priest in Vancouver, characteristic of stories we heard in other Catholic contexts, proclaimed, "In Vancouver I think we've got about 30 national parishes. You know like the Croatians, the Italians, the Poles, you know we've got about 30 different parishes that are about six Chinese parishes I think right now and Korean parish. So we emphasize more the cultural values of the people and once they come here they still have their own worshiping congregations and their languages and stuff. I think that's one thing that we're different that way." Part of the Canadian belief is that immigrants can "come as they are" without the need to necessarily or fully assimilate, which extends to congregational life. Of course, other congregations see the impact of immigration via multiethnic church settings – a theme we explore later.

A recurring refrain that we heard was that foreign-born Christians appear to be more conservative and countercultural to Canadian values than Canadian-born Christians. Some leaders went as far as to lament that Canadian-born Christians were not more countercultural and conservative in their religious attitudes and behaviours. An Anglican leader in Toronto shared:

> My congregation we have at least twenty-nine nations represented, and the people with the strongest biblical worldview are immigrants, they're not home-grown generally speaking. The people who are home-grown adopted the secular values and that's why we have the most liberal, abortion, lack abortion laws in the world as well, our stance on euthanasia plus a number of other items reflect a European secularism, born of the enlightenment so, you're dealing with

quite a wide range. When I go into social situations it's the home-grown born Canadian people who have the least biblical knowledge often. Particular if they're above forty years of age, and the school system of course is now socially engineering the next generation, so they'll be even further removed from any sort of biblical memory. If we understand that then our approach to mission needs to radically change … one of the problems for us as a denomination in Canada is we still haven't grasped the reality that the secular, agnostic, atheistic world view is now the predominant viewpoint. And so your approach to evangelism your approach to church growth radically has to change. It can't be by baptism, marriage, and osmosis, which is the historic kind of state church model of the Anglican Church.

A Catholic interviewee reinforced similar ideas, noting that Catholicism in Canada would struggle more deeply if it were not for immigration:

And right now the main thing in the Catholic Church is immigration. You know like the, in 10 years I think almost half a million Catholic immigrants and that's the reason why we're growing. Because the birth rate is going to flatten out pretty soon and so the immigrants is really what – and most of those immigrants that come, they have a strong devotional life. And the Pentecostal side is important or the Charismatic is – you know the whole thing of the various spiritual groups and that's really important I think in terms of people's personal faith. You know their relationship to Jesus kind of idea there. And they've got different interests or different ways of going at it but that's where they get their identity especially as far as their experience of God and their lives and the Holy Spirit and Christ.

Research is clear that in the foreseeable future religion in Canada, in many respects, will rise and fall on denominations and congregations' abilities to respond to the influx of Christian immigrants (Bibby & Reid 2016; Bramadat & Seljak 2008). We, of course, are very interested in the dynamics at work as congregations navigate and negotiate these changing demographics (we say more about this in our summary and discussion of how those in this study conceptualize flourishing congregations).

Few Churches are Large

Last, those who participated in phase one of this study noted that Canadian churches are generally smaller than their American counterparts. In some cases there is even a strong aversion to joining or growing large churches in Canada, possibly a reflection of our perceived "meek and mild" Canadian self-understanding. A Catholic leader in Halifax noted, "I would say a dynamic too of it and this isn't a Catholic- Protestant thing, but just smaller churches in general 'cause, you know, here's Halifax, a city of 400,000 plus whatever we are. We have no evangelical church over 1000 people. I don't know of where that would ever be the case in the U.S." Another leader in the Maritimes commented, "One of the things I always have to do when I'm reading sort of literature that comes specifically out of the U.S. is go 'we're not a country of mega churches.' Like that's not, for the most part, at least we in the United Church are not like hugely multi-staffed. Most of us are one with maybe some other paid support but not a lot. And so for me I think that's a very different piece."

Few Churches are Large

- Canadian churches generally smaller than in the United States (aversion toward large churches in some cases in Canada)

AMBROSE
UNIVERSITY

These leaders are partially correct. Recent estimates suggest there are approximately 150 Protestant churches in Canada with over 1000+ in weekly attendance versus 7,000 in the United States (Bird 2015). We do not have precise figures in the Catholic context, though all indications suggest this is where many of Canada's largest churches are located (Bibby & Reid 2016). Still, the majority of congregations on both sides of the border have congregations with fewer than one-hundred in weekly attendance. An intriguing observation about the source of growth in larger congregations arose in this quotation from a conservative Protestant pastor in Ontario that large congregations "are growing often at the expense of the smaller churches that are feeder churches of the bigger ones." This is certainly our hunch and our initial interviews and focus groups with leaders of larger congregations in Canada suggested that transfer growth is a key explanation for their numeric success. But we hope to gain greater clarity and precision about this and other realities based on church size in later stages of this study.

Conclusion

To conclude, congregations are impacted both by institutional and contextual factors. The purpose of this opening section was to present some of the contextual factors at play in the Canadian religious and cultural milieu, as perceived by participants in this study. In short, we heard that participants believe they are in a secular society; that religion and politics do not mesh well in the Canadian context; that Canadians value inclusivity and tolerance in a diverse and plural society; that Christians now operate from the margins of Canadian society; that cooperation rather than competition is highly esteemed; that immigration is believed to be a lifeline to Canadian congregations; and that few Canadian congregations are ostensibly large in weekly attendance. Together we think these views among leaders help to shape their conceptualization of what a flourishing congregation looks like, the subject of our next session. Importantly, most of the traits that we will discuss next deal with institutional variables. Yet we think these variables are very much conceptualized against the backdrop of some of the contextual variables highlighted thus far.

Section II

flourishing
CONGREGATIONS
INSTITUTE

Colleagues' Voices from Across Canada: Blog Collection

In this section, we gather the blogs written by our colleagues from across Canada and across the Catholic, mainline and conservative Protestant sectors. We continue to invite and publish blogs from academics, denominational and national leaders, as well as from local congregational leaders. Their insights and passion sets are obvious. In recognition of the launch of the Flourishing Congregation Institute, we felt there might be benefit to putting these blog contributions into this secondary format. We have ordered these contributions chronologically as they appeared on our website blog: http://www.flourishingcongregations.org/blog

Features of Flourishing Congregations

Dr. Joel Thiessen, Associate Professor of Sociology and Director of Flourishing Congregations Institute, Ambrose University

As our research team surveys the vast literature on churches that thrive, several interrelated features stand out. We note five of those features below, which are merely starters to an emerging conversation and research agenda connected to our newly formed Flourishing Congregations Institute, hosted at Ambrose University (Calgary, AB). What binds the following together is intentionality. Like cultivating habits in one's life, congregations do not flourish, develop, or thrive without intentionally seeking to do so.

Clear Self Identity: Flourishing congregations have a clear sense of who they are – where they come from, where they are now, and where they are going. They often learn from other churches along the way, yet they understand their uniqueness and do not strive to be like the others (e.g. how many Canadian churches have we encountered who mistakenly try to be like Willowcreek or Saddleback or any other American church). As part of knowing themselves, thriving churches involve many people and voices in the self-identity conversation – these are not solely concentrated among pastoral staff and board members. Leaders take time to listen to members in the congregation and to act upon the feedback that they receive, prioritizing clear, concise, and timely communication. The culmination of these variables are people who identify and buy-in to the congregation's identity and rally around the group's goals and mission, both in terms of financial and volunteer resources.

Leadership: Thriving churches equip and empower leaders to lead. Pastors are not all things to all people. They focus their responsibilities around their strengths and that specific congregation's needs, and they delegate lay leaders (it is key to identify and mobilize the right people for the right positions, rather than taking any willing body to fill a need) to play an instrumental role in the congregation's life. In this vein, flourishing congregations are generally set apart by pastors who stay a long time and take the time to build trust and rapport with members (research suggests that this truly begins to set in after five years). Encompassing all areas of leadership, flourishing groups strike the right balance between structure and flexibility in setting out strategies, making decisions, sharing authority, and so forth. These congregations are not so structured that they cannot make spur of the moment decisions along the way, but equally so, are not so open to any and all things that they have no underlying values and direction to orient their activities.

Culture that Desires Growth: Flourishing congregations have a cultural ethos that desires growth. These churches do not want to merely survive or remain static. Toward this end they commit to excellence in all things from quality of preaching, music, and programs, to treating people well. They encourage spiritual growth among members. Leaders and the congregation alike value learning, as a way to develop and broaden one's horizons toward effective ministry. These congregations are innovative and entrepreneurial, willing to take risks and make mistakes – however defined in their local context. Finally, thriving churches seek ongoing accountability and self-evaluation, with an eye toward improvement rather than living on past successes or failures.

Community: Churches that do well are known for inviting and welcoming people into a vibrant sense of belonging and participation. They create an environment where safety, love, acceptance, affirmation, and forgiveness are hallmark features of community life – and these traits are first and foremost spoken of and modeled by congregational leaders. Out of this focus ministries are generally relationship-centered, personal stories and testimonies are exchanged in different congregational-related gatherings. Once more, when people feel part of the faith community they are more likely to reciprocate with volunteering and financial resources … and the more that people attend and volunteer, the more likely they are to buy into the vision of that congregation.

Vibrant Spiritual Life: A commitment to a vibrant spiritual life is evident in flourishing churches. This includes teaching, opportunities, and resources that encourage members toward spiritual growth. Inspiring, engaging, and inspiring worship services are also common. A congregational commitment to sound stewardship of one's time, finances, talents, relationships, possessions, health, and knowledge is also key to churches that are doing well – this is mainly because it means that individuals and the congregation as a whole are generous toward others, rather than constantly self-serving (a common critique of churches). On this latter point, flourishing churches have a faith-based commitment to outreach and to serve those beyond the walls of their congregation. This entails an active evangelism focus, participation in various social justice initiatives, and an active presence in the community at large.

Our goal as a research group is to post two blogs a month on various topics related to flourishing congregations. We also plan to include other experts in this domain along with church leaders to provide helpful insights on this blog site. Have some ideas to contribute to this blog? Let us know ... and spread the word about this new and exciting research agenda!

Space and Place Speak

Dr. Bill McAlpine, Professor of Practical Theology, Ambrose University

In our first blog, Dr. Joel Thiessen outlined five aspects of flourishing congregations that will inform much of what we do together over the next few years of research and writing. Early in his blog, Joel made the following comment: "What binds the following together is intentionality. Like cultivating habits in one's life, congregations do not flourish, develop, or thrive without intentionally seeking to do so." If ever there was an element in the life of any congregation in which this is particularly true, it is in relation to the 'where' of the congregation, the place they meet, fellowship and worship as a body.

I am of the mind that this is particularly germane to the first aspect Joel mentioned, namely, a clear self-identity. A friend of mine, in a bout of friendly jousting once said to me, "Bill it doesn't matter where we worship, only that we worship." I assured him of my respect and for the fact that it was entirely within his prerogative to be wrong! A visitor or first-time attender to any church will have begun to assemble their understanding of who these people are well before any song is sung or sermon preached. In fact, this will begin before the first set of greeters is able to extend a warm handshake. People will read and interpret buildings before entering them. Yet unfortunately for many years and particularly within the evangelical world very little thought is typically given to what the buildings we design and construct might say to those we are hoping will attend. We are rightly concerned with what the building will do for us, but I am arguing that is not enough.

It is not difficult to show how far too many congregations have experienced the frustration generated by a built environment (either bought, built or borrowed/rented) that rather than facilitating the accomplishment of a vision or mission has in fact mitigated against it. The "where" of any flourishing congregation does matter! I understand the challenges of ministering in 'borrowed digs,' in situations when church plants, for example, meet in rented multi-purpose facilities such as town halls, gymnasiums or theatres. The omnipresence of God is not limited by the built environment. But to suggest, therefore, that the places where we gather as the Body of Christ are entirely inconsequential or at best secondarily important is to dangerously court a gnostic approach to spirituality.

Significantly, designers of shopping malls and restaurants seem to get it! They understand the effect of critical elements such as lighting, proportion and texture and they know that certain environments affect certain responses. As an example, the average fast food restaurant is designed to provide an environment that will be comfortable for the average patron for approximately 13 minutes. Hard, bold-coloured, seating, close proximity to other customers, and a loud acoustic ambiance all combine to discourage any undue lingering. By contrast other eating establishments with their soft, welcoming seating, subdued lighting, easy-listening music and often aromatic atmospheres are designed to foster and welcome visits of up to two or three hours. Elements such as generous amounts of natural light, running water and numerous lives plants have become very common features in more and more shopping malls.

According to a brochure I found in a world-renowned mega-mall, the proprietors do not want people to 'just shop' there; they want them to have 'an experience' which of course, will encourage them to stay longer and likely shop!

Should churches, then, work toward replicating such commercial spaces? No, not entirely. However, I am reminded of a phone interview I was privileged to have with a member of the management team at Willow Creek Community Church a number of years ago shortly after they had moved from their 4500 seat auditorium into their new 7200 seat gathering place. I asked the question what did they want people to do or experience when they entered their new space? The answer was immediate and concise: "First of all, we want attenders to slow down. Most of our people, living in the greater Chicago area endure rather frenetic lives from Monday to Friday. We have created a space that will allow indeed force them to slow down. Secondly, and most importantly, we want people to have an encounter with the living God, and thirdly, we want people to experience genuine community." My follow-up question was: "Are you saying that you believe that your new built environment has the capacity to facilitate or enhance those kinds of experiences?" The answer? "Without question! We have spent seven years in a detailed consideration of aspects such as lighting, material of seat cushions and seat backs, floor coverings, colors, knee space, sightlines and many more." Such efforts seem to be paying off!

Well, we may say, once again that is within a context south of the 49th parallel, in the United States! And that is true. It is for that reason that I am looking forward to listening with my colleagues to many experts and various stakeholders from a variety of church traditions within the Canadian context and testing my conviction that place and space speak; that the where of flourishing congregations does matter. In the meantime, let me encourage you to read my earlier book on the topic, Sacred Space for the Missional Church: Engaging Culture through the Built

Environment. I welcome your responses, and let us know what you think about this or other topics related to flourishing congregations.

The Place of Learning in a Flourishing Congregation

Dr. Arch Wong, Professor of Practical Theology, Ambrose University

As our research team began to survey the literature on flourishing congregations, one of the features that especially stood out for me centred on a vibrant spiritual life. A vibrant spiritual life is connected to discipleship. What does it mean to be a disciple? The Greek word for disciple is *mathetes,* which means a learner. To be a disciple is to be a learner.

Flourishing congregations seems to have a learning and teaching environment that fosters spiritual growth. However, when we think about teaching we often times think about preaching. Let me be clear: I do believe strongly in preaching and that it does have a component of teaching; what worries me is that for many church members, it is the only "spiritual food" that they eat and it is the only model of teaching that they have been exposed to.

Recently, I asked my seminary class if they remembered last week's sermon. About half of them did. I then asked them, did they remember what the pastor spoke about two weeks ago. Only a few hands went up. I then asked them, do you have any recollection of the pastor's sermon from six weeks ago. No hands went up. My point is this: despite its many limitations vis-à-vis learning, why do we continue to think that the transmission of information week after week is the only effective way of teaching for preachers, Sunday school teachers, or small group leaders? Why do disciples think that this is the only way to learn?

Mike Breen in his book, *Building a Discipling Culture*, argues for three ways of learning that interplay with one another: 1) Classroom/Lecture passing on of information; 2) Apprenticeship; and 3) Immersion. I agree with Breen and I can think of at least eight other teaching models that could be used in a congregation such as the nurturing, case study, or guided discovery models of teaching that are not exclusively information driven ways of learning for the disciple. I would venture to say that flourishing congregations have multiple ways of teaching and learning. For teachers, preachers, or mentors many of you have thought through the materials and researched the topic, but have you also given careful consideration to the learner in a classroom, small group, or one-on-one setting? For the learner, have you thought about how you best learn and is discipleship happening that best fits your learning style?

Some congregations have begun to take more seriously the different ways that people learn. Fleming and Baume (2006) have proposed four modalities of learning: visual, auditory, read and write, and kinesthetic (VARK). Although the research can be questioned, it does provide a heuristic way of understanding learning in the congregation. Learners use all four modalities for learning but one modality is normally more dominant. Visual learners like to see the words or prefer the use of images and graphic organizers to access and understand new information. Auditory learners best understand new content through listening and speaking in situations such as group discussions or lectures. Read and Write learners also like to see words and take notes and like to read. Kinesthetic learners like to be up and doing and best understand information through tactile representation of information.

So how might you engage different learners in a particular teaching and learning context? For example, if the teaching is on prayer, Visual and Read and Write learners would like written summaries or PowerPoints/Prezi with pictures, diagrams or charts. Auditory learners would much prefer conversations about prayer or providing feedback. Kinesthetic learners do not want to be given a lecture or a sermon about prayer, they want to get up and pray.

How does a congregation tackle the diverse learning style in a particular learning situations? There are many ways to do so but perhaps one way is to consider all four learning styles in a given teaching situation. I know what you are thinking: is this more work? The answer is yes. Will learning go up and increase in the congregation? Most likely.

As we embark on this multi-year flourishing congregations project, I wonder what a vibrant spiritual life in respect to learning may look like. My hunch is that these flourishing churches have multiple paths to teaching and learning. I welcome conversation and your thoughts and feedback on this matter or anything about flourishing congregations.

Is Flourishing a Fleeting Fad?

Dr. Keith Walker, Professor, University of Saskatchewan

> *Being healthy* AND FIT ISN'T *a fad or trend,* IT'S A LIFESTYLE.

The upright will flourish like the palm tree, will grow like the cedar of Lebanon. Planted in the house of Yahweh, they will flourish in the courts of our God. In old age they will still bear fruit, will remain fresh and green, to proclaim Yahweh's integrity; my role, in whom no fault can be found (Psalm 92:12-15, New Jerusalem Bible).

"Well, is this a fleeting fad, this flourishing stuff . . . Is this notion of flourishing just a new bumper-sticker for the same old?" I think this is a fair question in response to our use on this website and in our research of the phrase "flourishing congregations."

It is true that words such as vibrant, vital, thriving, alive, healthy, happy, well-being, blessed, proliferative, successful, prosperous and burgeoning have witnessed a renaissance in our more recent rhetoric and lexicons of description when we want to describe and imagine (out loud) what we'd like to see more of in congregations. It is a rather welcome break from the PLOMS dis-ease (or the tragic "Poor Little Old Me" Syndrome) that so frequently plagues those of us who love Jesus Christ and His Church.

The healthy skeptic's imputation of this phrase that it is merely marketing or branding garnish may understandable but a further examination of the motivations of users is warranted. In a literal sense "to flourish" has meant to "flower," to "lengthen the stem," or to "grow vigorously or profusely." Right off the bat, I would say that we are less interested in neologisms, denotation and connotations than we are in manifestations. For us there are a variety of meanings on spectra of: ideal to real, subjective to objective, intuitive to empirical, natural to supernatural, material to spiritual, metaphysical to phenomenal.

Put simply, we are on a search to bring description to what is working in congregations – giving wide-berth to seeing the unexpected, to observing the predictable, to hearing the witnesses of miracles (i.e., God doing what God chooses to do), to observing common sense and good old fashion hard work in action, to puzzling with synchronicity (apparent acausality), to rejigging our various stipulative and assumptive definitions and to doing some deep learning from the situated experiences and traditions of other Christians and those wired different than us.

Ancient to contemporary commentators enthusiastically chime in for our edification: From Aristotle's notion eudaemonia (happiness), as living our lives in the company of friends in accordance to our most commended and habituated virtues (Book 10 of Nicomachean Ethics), to indexes of Canadian wellbeing (https://uwaterloo.ca/canadian-index-wellbeing/about-canadian-index-wellbeing), to the contributions of burgeoning fields such as positive psychology (i.e., subjective well-being) and positive organizational studies (i.e., positive deviance), to the plethora of Church growth books offering lists, and more lists, of features, qualities, attributes, and characteristics that are root and fruit of healthfulness, together with the best and latest homily or sermon on being the prevailing Church. We are allowing ourselves to play in an array of conceptual sandboxes but our strong urge is to enter into the life-worlds of congregations and leaders across Canada and to join our senses with those of our partners to make good sense of what we are able to learn from each other.

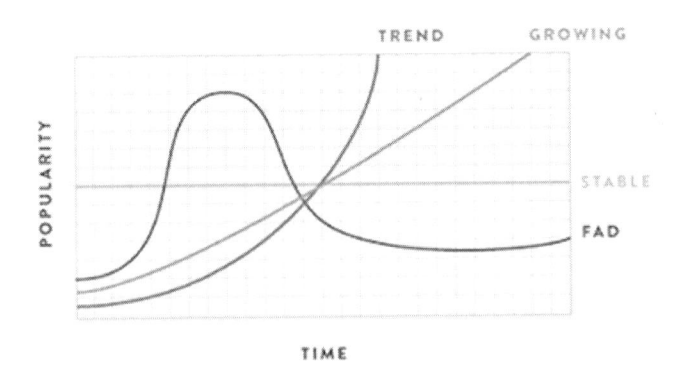

[Graph with vertical axis labeled POPULARITY and horizontal axis labeled TIME, showing curves labeled TREND, GROWING, STABLE, and FAD]

Given this, we are using the phrase "flourishing congregations" for a wide-open range of possibilities that privilege our noticing what God is doing and what His people are experiencing across Canada. Yes, we admit to being tired and worn down by deficit language in conversations about the dire state of the Church. I'd suggest this inquiry of ours isn't so much a "same-old, same-old thing" (though, as demonstrated above, the allied notions of flourishing have been with us for a long time). We do not have in mind developing a set of new clichés or simply putting on a store-bought wardrobe to hide an old and atrophic body. Neither is it about hopping onto a new fad's bandwagon with adjectival sizzle to reify fading glory or to prop up organizational nominalism. No

– I suggest that for us - this is a "flip of the switch" that permits us, against our propensities or tendencies to "bad-finding" and self-critique, to see ourselves at our contextual or situated best rather than beating ourselves, and others, up. This is a call for us to be mutual witnesses of our flourishing congregational lives as we bring to description the root attitudes and actions that give rise to God-glorifying communities of faith, across Christian traditions in Canada. This research encourages us to tilt our sights to what we imagine it would be like to experience more and more of what God loves and what we were made to delight in.

For us, the joy in this journey will be the presence of the Lord and our ever-welcome co-journeyers.

Flourishing Congregations Are Well Managed and Effectively Governed

Dr. Gordon T. Smith, President and Professor, Ambrose University

It is not uncommon for pastors to bemoan administrative work as a necessary evil that no doubt has to be done, but which if they had their druthers would not take up any time or energy. Sometimes what is typically called "administration" is viewed as a problem – an obstacle to true religious leadership and pastoral care. And, consequently, many pastors have never developed their organizational or institutional capacities. The most influential pastoral theologian of our generation – Eugene Petersen – is just one example, but an influential example, of this way of thinking. Peterson does not at any point in his key contributions to the vocation of pastoral ministry consider or speak to what it means to work with the board, the denominational bodies, the finances and the budget and the other institutional aspects of congregational life.

Disparaging administration and governance is almost viewed to be a badge of honour, reflecting that a pastor is slightly more spiritual, more true to calling and thus somehow above it all.

And yet for so many pastors the biggest challenges and greatest source of stress will come precisely at this point: the institutional character of congregations. Yes, of course, a congregation is not only an institution. And yet, could it be that a congregation – a local church – will never thrive without attention to the institutional dimension of the church? And could it be that this is not a distraction or necessary evil but actually integral to true pastoral ministry – just like the attention to personal well-being necessarily means attention to the health of our bodies? And could it be that a pastor's best efforts in other dimensions of ministry will be for naught if the congregation is not effectively managed and governed?

Could it be that Petersen's discounting of administration reflects a one-sided view of congregational life and ministry? Could it be that administration and thus administrative capacities are essential if our theological vision for the church will find concrete and tangible expression in the practices that make it possible for a congregation to flourish? That, indeed, many congregations never do flourish for the very simple reason that the fundamental administrative structures and procedures have not been put in place and followed.

The authors of *The Trellis and the Vine*, Collin Marshall and Tony Payne (Matthias Midia, 2009), in speaking of pastoral ministry make a distinction between the basic work of the ministry – the proclamation of the Gospel and the care for people – and what they speak of as the "framework" that is so crucial if the ministry is to grow. They put it this way: "as the ministry grows, the trellis also needs attention. Management, finances, infrastructure, organization, governance – these all become more important and more complex as the vine grows."

I would go further and stress that in actual fact attending to the institutional character of congregational life is "basic work" and vital to the ministry of the church. Pastors long to make a difference – to be catalysts for substantive change in their congregations – not merely in numbers, but also in the emotional, spiritual vitality of their faith communities and their missional impact within their neighborhoods and communities. And my point is that long term, substantive impact requires the "basic work" of attending to what Payne and Marshall call the framework: questions of good governance, effective personnel policies and practices, financial resilience and strategic initiatives and partnerships. Effective pastors get this.

Canadian Church Leaders Speak Out on Vision

Rev. Dr. Don Moore, National Church Ambassador, World Vision Canada

Who's responsible for vision in the church? How do you create and communicate vision? What difference does vision make? Through a recent national study, 227 church leaders revealed their perspective on how they see vision in ministry today. This study was done by the Church Engagement team at World Vision Canada last fall. Let's take a closer look at the responses to each of these three questions.

Leaders cast vision: 63% of respondents believe it's the role of leadership (pastoral staff and board) to create the vision statement. However there is a difference of opinion based on denominations.

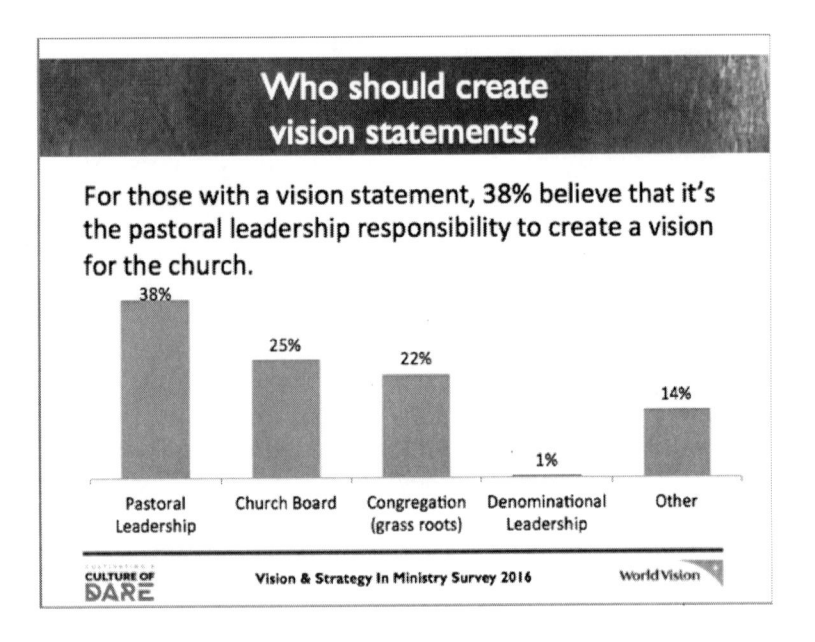

Who should create vision statements?

For those with a vision statement, 38% believe that it's the pastoral leadership responsibility to create a vision for the church.

- Pastoral Leadership: 38%
- Church Board: 25%
- Congregation (grass roots): 22%
- Denominational Leadership: 1%
- Other: 14%

CULTURE OF DARE — Vision & Strategy In Ministry Survey 2016 — World Vision

Mainline denominations believe it's primarily the role of the congregation to develop the vision whereas evangelical denominations place emphasis on the role of church leadership. Either way, the important thing is to have as wide spread ownership of the vision by as many as possible. How have you worked with your leaders and your people in creating vision?

Create then communicate: 41% of leaders identify creating a compelling vision statement and communicating that vision as the most challenging steps in the process of creating vision and strategy.

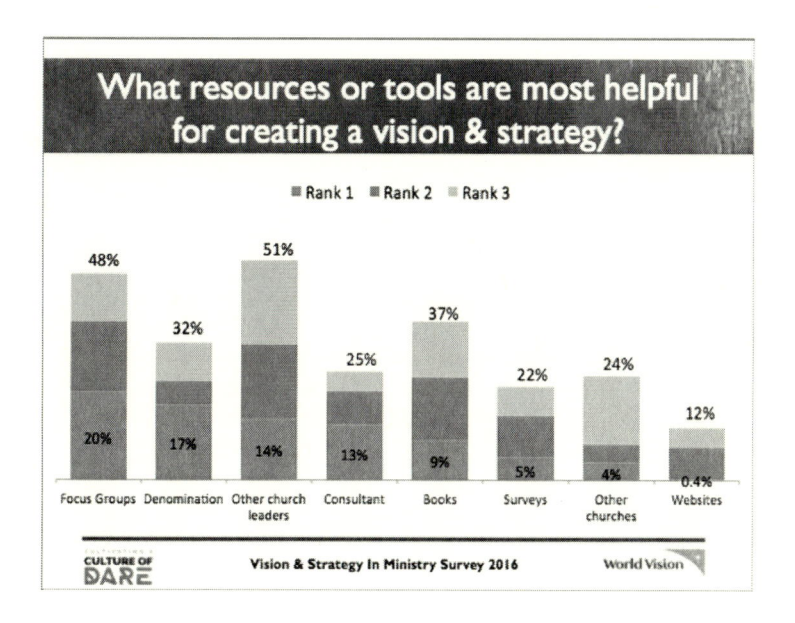

What resources or tools are most helpful for creating a vision & strategy?

Rank 1 | Rank 2 | Rank 3

- Focus Groups: 48% (Rank 1: 20%)
- Denomination: 32% (Rank 1: 17%)
- Other church leaders: 51% (Rank 1: 14%)
- Consultant: 25% (Rank 1: 13%)
- Books: 37% (Rank 1: 9%)
- Surveys: 22% (Rank 1: 5%)
- Other churches: 24% (Rank 1: 4%)
- Websites: 12% (Rank 1: 0.4%)

Vision & Strategy In Ministry Survey 2016 — CULTURE OF DARE / World Vision

Getting your message heard is always a challenge for leaders. The more channels of communication both formal and informal that can be used the better.

How well articulated is your vision? How many channels of communication do you use? What others might be considered?

Walking the talk: 72% of leaders say their day-to-day church ministry is moderately or extremely aligned with their church vision. This suggests that vision statements are an effective tool for focusing ministry and mission.

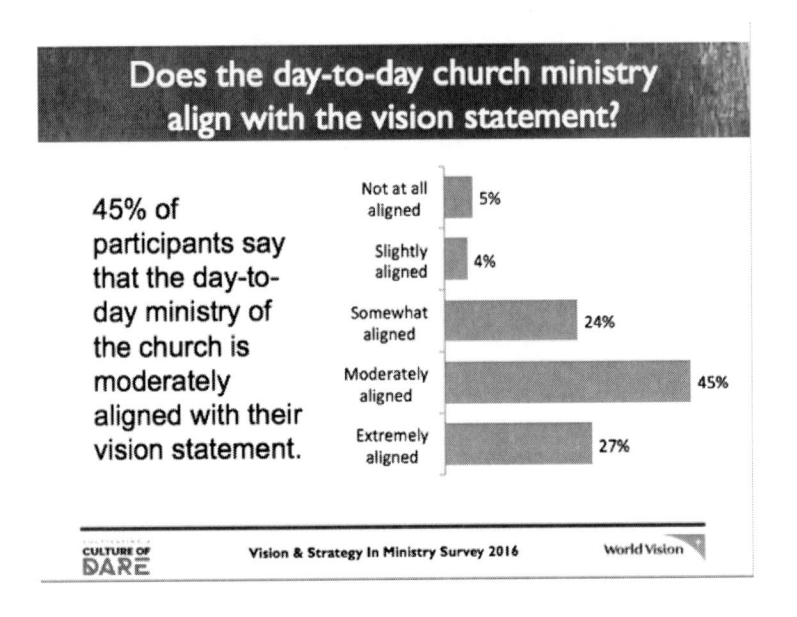

Does the day-to-day church ministry align with the vision statement?

45% of participants say that the day-to-day ministry of the church is moderately aligned with their vision statement.

Alignment	Percentage
Not at all aligned	5%
Slightly aligned	4%
Somewhat aligned	24%
Moderately aligned	45%
Extremely aligned	27%

CULTURE OF DARE — Vision & Strategy In Ministry Survey 2016 — World Vision

It's important to recognize that the greater the alignment of each facet of ministry, the greater the likelihood that your church vision will be achieved. How do you work to bring about alignment in your ministry?

Daring to Dream: I believe vision is all about tapping into the potential and the dreams that God has given you, as a church leader, to make a difference in the world through the mission of your local church.

People tend to rally around a leader who has a clear sense of purpose and direction. Vision is very motivating. It gives meaning and significance to why you exist. It provides a clear sense of direction.

Vision gives you the opportunity to bring about changed lives and make a difference for the sake of the Kingdom. As a church, you have the potential ability to become an invaluable neighbour in your community.

My prayer is that these findings may spark a conversation around vision for ministry that might inspire some new creative thinking around how we do effective and vibrant ministry today.

More findings from this study on Vision & Strategy are available on the World Vision Church Engagement website: http://churches.worldvision.ca/.

*The above mentioned study was prepared for the Annual Church Leaders Forums currently being held entitled, "Cultivating a Culture of Dare: Ministry Vision and Strategy" being hosted in 12 major cities across Canada. The World Vision Canada Church Engagement (NCE) team aims to work alongside churches equipping and encouraging them to live out God's mission to serve those living in poverty and with injustice.

Three Suggestions for the Shifting Economy of Church

Jeremy Duncan, Lead Pastor at Kensington Commons Church, Calgary

It is an interesting time for churches in Canada. My sense is that after decades of slow decline we are at a liminal point in our trajectory. This is not a doom and gloom scenario that I see on the horizon but instead a point of reflection and change that can help the larger church move into her emerging role in a post-christian Canada.

There is much to be said about this transition and the lessons we will need to learn as we move forward but I'd like to highlight one particular area from my perspective as a church planter; the economics of church.

I tend to approach church from within the framework I was handed in the Evangelical tradition. Though I have learned greatly from the mainline perspectives in the past decade many of the concepts I see perpetuated in the church planting movement today tend to rely on the economic models that have been enjoyed in evangelicalism for the past several decades. That is, a built-in presumption of generosity that is funnelled primarily through the church. This has allowed churches to build around program-heavy, staff-resourced, facility-driven models. One study from Christianity Today in 2013 found that the average North American Evangelical church consumes 97% of all their resources on internal programming such as personnel and facility.

Today's millennials are, in my experience, no less generous than the previous generation but there are two factors that dramatically impact their financial relationship with churches.

First, millennials do not see the church as the default recipient for their generosity. They are willing to contribute to communities they are a part of but that does not mean that their church community will be the sole beneficiary of what they may see as their spiritual, humanitarian, and civic donations. Church will be, one of many outlets for generosity. Compounding this is a built skepticism that many hold toward the church, or even charities, in general. Millennials expect a level of transparency that many churches are simply not ready to provide. A church that does not appear generous in their use of resources will probably have a tough time attracting the generosity of millennials.

Secondly, millennials are facing an economic climate over the next few decades where traditional sources of wealth creation will likely not provide the same returns. The housing market, where many boomers have considerable wealth invested, probably cannot sustain the same trajectory it has enjoyed since the 1950s. This means churches will need to survive off of generosity funded through disposable income rather than accumulated wealth.

None of this serves as a death knell–resources will still be there for churches who can adapt–it is simply part of the economic reality of church today. Churches who build from traditional expectations about giving patterns will have a tough time becoming sustainable in the long term and church planting networks would do well to not perpetuate these models by pumping in large infusions of cash early in the planting cycle.

A few suggestions:

1. Church plants will need to have long term rental plans or partnership strategies where they work with existing churches. Capital heavy facility plans are probably not realistic in this climate. One of the most compelling opportunities we have in Canada is to see churches that reach end-of-life, partner with emerging communities to provide facility resources.

2. Churches will need to focus on becoming decentralized with a community volunteer focus taking precedence over staffing. Bi-vocational models have long been employed in the church and a return is likely necessary in many cases. Churches who envision themselves as small organic communities serving less than a hundred people in a tight community can be powerful pockets of kingdom life but the resources of full-time staff may not be realistic in those environments. Plans will need to adapt accordingly. Even larger churches will need to think about shifting

resources toward empowering community ministry over programmatic models that require a heavy staff presence.

3. Churches will need to have clear generosity initiatives where they model the kind of sacrificial giving that they want to teach their communities. The kind of kingdom generosity that makes church possible is no longer going to be powered by social pressure the way it has been in the past. This means that teaching–primarily through demonstration rather than talking points–will be a necessary element of our discipleship.

Eugene Peterson is fond of saying that, "The vocation of pastor has been replaced by the strategies of religious entrepreneurs with business plans." He is on to something here. However, as I see it, what he is taking aim at is not the result of the kind of analysis I'm proposing. His critique is the result of trying to maintain the status quo in a shifting economic environment. When we can only think of doing church with the massive financial resources we have become accustomed to, we are forced to turn church into a business model designed to raise capital. When we can honestly evaluate the local economy around us and dream up sustainable models that work naturally within that context, we can get back to doing the work of ministry without having to focus on propping up our bottom line.

To Flourish, Congregations must be Emotionally Healthy

Rev. Clara King, St. George's Anglican Church, Rural Missioner for the Anglican Diocese of Calgary

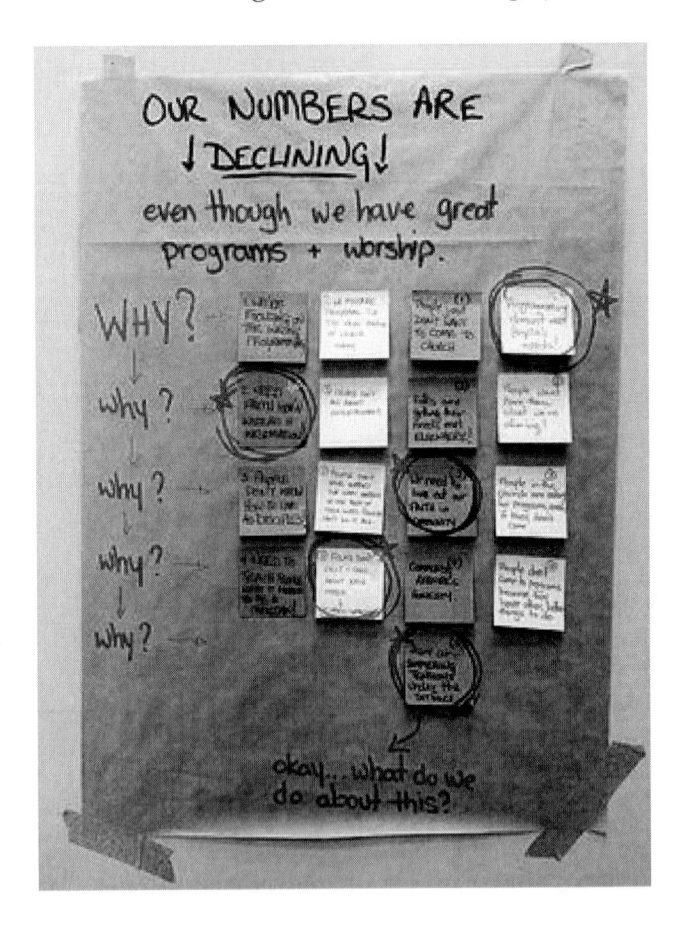

The other day, I found myself hearing yet another story of a congregational development effort that had gone wrong. My colleague had done everything right, according to a well-tested

program, but somehow things still went badly wrong. Looking back, he said, "I should have noticed that all their previous pastors had been ousted under odd circumstances." In the end, that's exactly what happened to him too.

At least my colleague is not alone. Situations like this happen all the time in church-land: a good program fails when it's brought face to face with the actual, real-life people of a congregation.

There are thousands of programs to make a congregation awesome, so why is it that some congregations are able to flourish, while others, despite all the best programs and intentions in the world, simply don't?

This is not only a Church question. Over the past decade or so, the Harvard Business School Press has published a lot of books on the theme of "why are some organizations so creative and adaptable and others aren't?" The answer? It seems that Edwin Friedman was right (*Generation to Generation*, 1985): there are underlying emotional dynamics that affect everything that happens in any given community - a business, a corporation, or even a congregation. Now, Friedman's intellectual successors (like Ron Heifetz & Marty Linsky) are giving us new insights and resources to understand organizations better

When emotional dynamics are healthy, organizations are vibrant, creative, risk-taking and highly adaptable, being able to meet any challenge with ease while retaining the essence of their identity. When the emotional dynamics are poor, organizations are rigid and reactive, trying to ignore or dismiss the need for change, and unable to cope with conflict.

We've all seen this in congregational life. Some congregations are places of incredible creativity, adaptability and risk-taking in service of the Gospel. Other congregations fracture over disproportionately small issues. I heard once of a church that lost 20 families because the Sanctuary was given a new coat of paint in the same colour. The situation didn't get any better once those people had left: the toxic emotional dynamic underlay the entire congregation.

This gives us an additional set of diagnostic tools for understanding congregational vitality. Whether a congregation has 20 or 2,000 parishioners, we can ask: are there small issues that are blown out of proportion? (Teacups seem to be a contentious focal point in many Anglican parishes!). Are there repeated negative patterns in the congregation's history, particularly moments of fracture? How has the congregation dealt with major change before? Has the congregation been able to compromise to heal a conflict?

More than average Sunday attendance and the state of the balance sheet, these diagnostic tools help us understand a congregation's vitality. They'll affect whether a new program will work, whether people will leave because of conflict, whether the congregation can adapt to whatever changes will come its way in the future. In order to flourish, congregations must be emotionally healthy.

Beyond "Love It or List It"

Rev. Joel S. Den Haan, Principal, Joel Den Haan Consulting Group

In my work as a consultant for mission and capital planning I have become drearily familiar with the church version of a popular real estate show, "Love It or List It."

Some congregations hunker down in their cherished but decaying facilities, renting derelict empty space out to anyone who'll take it in a pattern reminiscent of the tenement landlords in Charles Dickens' England. The members keep gathering in smaller and smaller groups, disconnected from the community around them and fundraising to keep the lights on until the last one passes away.

Other congregations take a quicker path to demise: having exhausted their energies on building upkeep, they throw in the towel and list their property for sale to whoever wants to buy it. The result is visible in many urban centres across the country: facilities for public worship and neighbourhood ministry sold off and converted into "unique private condominium lifestyles" suited only for people of means.

I have come to believe that neither of these two scenarios represent the best stewardship of the land and economic assets our forebears in the faith have passed on to us. Not only is the value of these assets degraded through the "Love It or List It" approach - we also sacrifice genuine opportunities to respond to the Gospel call within changed communities around us. The Good News is still needed, still life-giving in the places our church facilities are located, and by choosing to either hunker down or bail out we eliminate for ourselves the opportunity to live the Gospel in a new day.

Congregations and communities deserve a better approach than "Love It or List It". That's why I have developed the Three Circles model for evaluating and revitalizing congregational community mission.

Think back to your Middle School math class, and the Venn Diagram the teacher used to help explain the properties of numbers. Our Three Circles approach works a similar way: in the first circle, we consider the unique faith identity of your congregation, its values, its heritage, the special traditions that give meaning to congregational life. The second circle takes in the community context - an honest appraisal of the social agencies, businesses, community and municipal structures, and neighbourhood relationships around your church facility. And then, in the final circle of the three, we consider the facility and land assets themselves - what are the regulatory and economic factors that impact church property, and what possibilities exist for new missional purposes in your location?

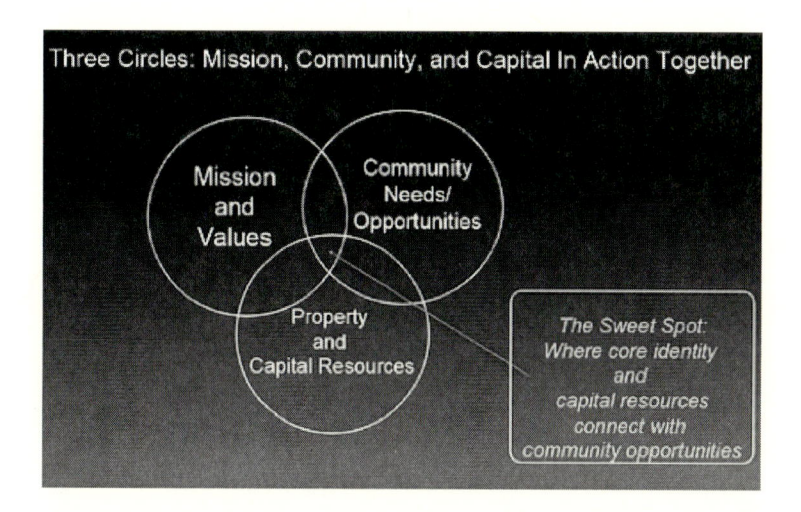

> **Three Circles: Mission, Community, and Capital In Action Together**
>
> - Mission and Values
> - Community Needs/Opportunities
> - Property and Capital Resources
>
> *The Sweet Spot: Where core identity and capital resources connect with community opportunities*

At the intersection of the Three Circles, we can identify the point where your congregation's character and legacy connect with the community around you, to allow new ways to deploy your assets faithfully and effectively. My work with a number of congregations has shown me that a Three Circles approach can open up new directions for mission and ministry effectiveness that would never come to life if we're simply thinking "Love It or List It."

Giving It Up For Rent

Rev. Joel S. Den Haan, Principal, Joel Den Haan Consulting Group

We've talked about how clarifying your congregation's mission and identity, combined with intentionally re-connecting with the community around you, can reveal new pathways toward thriving ministry.

As we move down those pathways, we may need to leave behind past patterns, and think in new ways about how we steward the legacy of our church property and assets. One of those patterns is something a lot of congregations have taken on over the years: building rentals. We're all familiar with how it works: churches who no longer use all their space, and who can't afford the upkeep on their own, decide to take their space and make it available to anyone who will pay for it. And in this way, congregations begin the shift from being in the "mission" business, to being in the "landlord" business - whether they want to or not.

There are at least three reasons why I don't like to see churches become landlords on any kind of large scale:

> **A.** Rentals form a crutch of financial denial: Increased rental revenues allow congregations to mask the financial realities that arise when donations and mission capacity start to decline. We can pretend we're still viable, even thriving, because the operating statement seems to balance. But underneath, the disconnect between our ministry priorities and the mission opportunities around us grows larger.

> **B.** Rentals can make change more difficult. For example, a congregation I know in a new, growing community rented out a large portion of its recently-constructed facility space. A large, paying tenant moved in, helping the church pay down its mortgage. The trouble arose when both the tenant and the congregation needed to expand their utilization of church space: the only path for the congregation to grow lay in kicking the tenants out. In the process, a long-term lease, as well as a good deal of community goodwill, were sacrificed, simply in order to allow the congregation to grow into its own space. Further, the congregation suddenly faced a cash flow crunch, as the rental income evaporated before regular givings rose to fill the gap. Surely this wasn't

the intention behind building the facility in the first place!

C. Renting is not a Gospel value: this is actually the biggest reason I would like to see congregations get out of the landlord business. Churches, pure and simple, are not meant to be in the business of setting up commercial landlord/ tenant agreements. Churches are intended to be places where people develop genuine, caring relationships with one another first and foremost. And exchanging rent cheques for use of space is actually a way we set an arms'-length distance between one another.

In my experience, thriving congregations don't make a practice of depending on rental income from their facilities. Thriving churches avoid the trap of relying on rental revenue to compensate for mission weakness.

Instead, thriving congregations focus first and foremost on their mission and direction in response to the Good News. They do ministry that matters within their community, and they deploy their facilities and their resources to support those things that really matter.

The Practices of a Flourishing Rural Church

Dr. Tim Beadle, Co-Founder of Rural Church Pastors Network & Church Effectiveness Coach

While over eighty percent of Canada's population live in urban centers, 90% of our diverse landscape is ministered to by rural pastors and their church families. Often misunderstood and definitely underappreciated, rural churches go about their ministries faithfully serving their regions without notice nor fanfare. While many may reduce rural churches to small, second class and behind the times, nothing could be further from the flourishing truth!

Throughout the country, the pulse of rural ministry is infused with both joy and challenge! The extent to which they can celebrate and navigate through life and shifting economic realities and cultural expressions finds within the fabric of their faith an ability to flourish. So what does a flourishing rural church actually look and feel like?

The metrics used to 'measure' this experience in rural life however are not the traditional ones used across the board by denominations. The standards of 'butts, bucks, and buildings' don't apply to this unique sphere of ministry. Rather, more qualitative expressions are those within which expressions of flourishing rural churches can be found.

Understanding context is primary in understanding the essence of rural life and ministry. Church families experience the living and ever-changing backdrop of nature through which they sense the ongoing presence of the God they worship. Be it the majestic mountains, the rolling prairies, the glistening lakes or fragrant forests, flourishing rural ministry is tethered to the land in which believers share their lives and experience their faith together.

Relationships are the primary vehicle through which rural churches flourish. Congregations thrive to the extent they care for each other and share true biblical fellowship and discipleship. Due to the smaller size of their communities, their need for relational interconnectedness is vital. Churches that flourish display ongoing signs of congregational life that goes far beyond surface relationships into the fabric of a shared life and faith experience. Such relationships represent the vital lifeline that allows church families to bond and flourish together.

Some may say this is true of all churches, and I have no problem in agreeing. However understanding the interconnected nature of rural life makes the ability to living in relational harmony more challenging. Rural folk 'live together' for good or bad, through thick and thin. They share life with each other continually throughout the week – at the gas station, the coffee shop, the school and grocery store. Their experience of church isn't what happened the previous Sunday in the sanctuary. Rather, it is found in the down to earth experience of living collectively within the context of their faith in communities that are driven by the demands and rhythms of the land upon which they live.

Life experience in a flourishing rural church proceeds at a slower pace of life and living compared to the 'rat race' of urban reality and it isn't because rural residents don't have a lot to do. People make time for each other to talk life and family, not just business. Because church life is shared holistically and experienced intergenerationally, the priority given to the 'family' is deemed central to all of church life. This is seen in people looking out for each other's kids, and where teens are trained to be strong church leaders with the expectation of using their gifts and talents as a part of their worshipping community.

Finally, a flourishing rural church looks past their lack of resources and creates a God honouring expression of 'church life' by putting to use the full extent of spiritual gifts and physical talents present within the body of Christ. The level of investment in a flourishing church is therefore very high, not only because of the need to get involved because of lack of numbers, but as an expression of a living faith in which God has called them into ministry and service for the common good of the community. This means every flourishing rural church is quite unique in and of itself depending on the mix of people who not only fill the pews, but who also share their lives together.

When was your 'God-Moment'?

Fr. Jerome Lavigne, Pastor of St. Peter's Roman Catholic Church, Calgary

There's an Executive Headhunter out there who has a unique style when it comes to finding and recruiting corporate executives for large firms. The first thing he likes to do when he's conducting the interview is disarm the potential recruit: "I offer him a drink, take off my coat, undo my tie, throw my feet up on the desk and talk about Baseball, Football, Family, whatever the case may be – until he's all relaxed. Then, when I think I've got him relaxed, I lean over and I look him square in the eye and say: 'So, tell me – what's your purpose in life?'"

"It's amazing how top executives fall apart at that question." But then one day, something else happened... He had this one potential candidate completely disarmed with his feet up on the desk talking about football. The headhunter leaned in for the kill: "So, what's your purpose in life?"

Without blinking an eye, the Executive leaned in towards him and replied: "To go to heaven and take as many people with me as I can." "For the first time in my career," said the headhunter, "I was the one who was speechless..."

While there might be 1000 great ideas out there concerning what needs to happen in order to make a congregation flourish in our day and age, it's all smoke and mirrors unless those who've walked through the front door of your church are there because through the ministry entrusted to your care, you have served them in such a way, that you have made it possible for them to have a God moment realization: gotta get to heaven!

God moments are the power for change in the world. A church without God moments is like a ship without a rudder tossing about until it gets caught in the seaweed. Thing is, it's not about the magic program, it's not about the comfortable seats and the relaxed atmosphere: it's about the Pastor's own quest for the heart of God exemplified through holiness of life. It's about those in leadership positions within the church living out their day to day ever mindful of their own God moments.

St. Alphonsus de Liguori captures it best: "a torch that is not inflamed, cannot light the way." After all, it's one thing to be Christian by name, just like it's one thing to be a soldier who's not on the battlefield. It's another thing to live out the love that burns in one's heart for Jesus Christ by the power of His Spirit in order to bring all glory to God the Father just like it's another thing to be a soldier in the front lines pinned down to the ground amidst a rainstorm of crossfire.

Every adult Christian worth their salt has had a good number of God moments throughout the course of their life journey. The world would have us believe that it was a 'coincidence', an experience subject to our own interpretation of reality. But those of true Faith know otherwise. Flourishing congregations happen because Pastors read themselves full, think themselves clear, pray themselves hot, and let themselves go! Potential God moments in the life of a congregation are born out of a living witness.

Pastors, church leaders, all in authority within any given church – pass on the gift of Faith alive in your heart to those around you so that by means of your witness, they will come to discover the only purpose in life that really matters. Next time someone asks you why you do what you do; share with them the ultimate purpose of life. "My purpose in life is to go to heaven and take as many people with me as I can . . . " for all else is dust and air.

God Doesn't Always Say 'Go'!

Todd Petkau, Lead Pastor, Riverwood Church Community, Winnipeg

I'm a pretty active guy. Can't sit still. Always on the go. So, I love preaching Genesis 12:1 and Matthew 28:19! These verses provide the most concise sermon title, which just happens to double as the application: "GO!" After all, God commanded Abraham to 'pack up and get moving' and Jesus commanded all of us to 'shake off our tendency to settle and move on', right? Our assumption is that we'll flourish when we move. So you can imagine the surprise when we felt like God was saying "Don't go!"

Our story was somewhat typical. Plant a church in a rented junior high school. Move equipment in and out every weekend for five years before gathering enough resources to purchase a building in a part of town where the property was cheap. Spend a year of volunteer labour renovating a 30 year old door factory into a church. Move in. Outgrow the space. Plan on building a bigger building!

This is where life became a bit more complicated for us. We were now a 14 year-old church that was making an impact in the community. We were mowing lawns, replacing roofs, cleaning up the streets, distributing food, partying in the park, caring for the vulnerable and under-resourced and living out the gospel in our community. However, there were no old buildings or vacant lots that would accommodate the new 1000-1200 seat auditorium we thought we needed. So, we began looking outside of our community, in the suburbs where the land is plentiful and the parking lots are big.

That's when we heard "Don't go!" Our response was more of a protest. "Fine! We'll stay. But how are we supposed to grow? There is no property big enough to accommodate us!"

Over the next few years we stumbled on two short phrases that would radically change our perspective and form the launching pad for a novel approach to growing a church.

The first rolled off the lips of Larry Osborne, lead pastor of North Coast Church in San Diego: "Leaders like it big, but people like it small!" Something leapt inside of us when we first heard this statement. Not only did it seem to resonate with truth, but it also gave us permission to start looking for smaller venues rather than one large one.

The second phrase came out of our study of Acts 2:42 and was captured in just two words: "More small." This grammatically awkward little phrase formed the battle cry for our church. We would grow and expand our influence by becoming 'more small'.

Armed with a new perspective on church expansion we looked at our community with some fresh eyes. To our surprise, we found 28,000 sq ft of potential ministry space available to us in two old buildings sitting less than a block away! One was a 100 year old fire hall and the other a 6000 sq. ft. warehouse.

It's been a long journey and we're still in the 'experimental phase', but two months ago we became a church with six worship communities in three worship venues all within a block of each other. Each worship community currently runs between 80 and 400 people, but for the first time in years we have empty seats with room to invite friends and grow. Best of all, we're watching as people are connecting better because of these strategically smaller worship environments.

There is no doubt that staying has been much more demanding than it would have been for us to go! We've had to think harder, plan better (which we're not very good at!) and keep reminding ourselves why we're doing what we're doing a lot more. Thankfully, we've stumbled on a third little mantra that fuels our resolve: "Do hard things!"

When faced with a challenge, we experienced just how easy it is to default to conventional church wisdom and just how unconventional some of God's answers can be.

The Church as a City of Refuge

Mark Buchanan, Associate Professor of Pastoral Theology, Ambrose Seminary

This June, my wife and I visited the village of La Chambon sur Lignon, in the mountains of France near the borders of Switzerland and Italy. It is small hamlet in a remote place, surrounded by deep valleys and dense forests, with a shallow reedy river bending through it. It is far from any major centre.

Which was what made La Chambon perfect for its one claim to historical significance: it was the only community in Europe that sheltered Jews during WWII. There were individuals who did that. There were organizations that did so as well. Two countries, Denmark and Bulgaria, took heroic stands against Nazi deportation of Jews. But La Chambon alone worked together as an entire community to protect Jewish people, as many as would come, from the tragic fate that otherwise awaited them under the Vichy regime of France.

Altogether, the villagers saved over 5000 Jewish men, women and children – mostly children, who not only survived but who received a first-class education during those years.

Why did this single community act this way? At the centre of La Cambon, figuratively and literally, was a church, and at heart of that church was a pastor, Andre Trocme. Trocme, along with his formidable wife Magda and his faithful associate Edouard Theis, forged the vision for what La Chambon could be, and then through their preaching and leadership persuaded the entire community to put everything at risk for the sake of total strangers. It was remarkable feat, though the people of La Chambon, so grounded in the gospel through Trocme's preaching and their own deep roots of faith, nurtured by centuries of suffering, didn't think they were doing anything extraordinary.

Isn't this what all Christians do? That's how they saw it.

We were deeply moved to visit the place. We walked to the eastern edge of town where the railway line still exists that in the 1940s carried to the village hundreds of Jewish children, sent by parents in a last desperate attempt to save them. I tried to imagine those children, alone, frightened, weary, embraced by the robust welcome and generosity and courage of the Chambonais. Many of those children later said those were the best years of their lives.

Because of a church. Because of a pastor.

Today, the home where the Trocmes once lived is no more than a memorial. And the church where Andre preached has suffered the fate of so many of the churches of Europe – an old building where only a few, mostly elderly, folks still gather.

The lessons here are both inspiring and sobering. Without that church, without its leaders, La Chambon would have likely been no different from all the other communities throughout Europe – perhaps personally opposed to Nazi policies, but not inclined to put their own welfare at risk for the sake of strangers. But because of that church, and its leaders, La Chambon made a literal world of difference for over 5000 people. And, I imagine, it transformed the hosts and much as the guests.

And yet the church's vitality didn't survive much beyond its moment of crisis or the succession of its leadership. Maybe, given the remoteness of the village and the general drift of Christianity in post-war Europe, the church's diminishment was inevitable.

But I'd like to think it wasn't. I'd like to think that the vision that the church rose to and that the community rallied around – to be a City of Refuge, a place of welcome and generosity and courage for frightened and weary and lonely people, to be the welcoming arms of Christ himself – is still the call of the church here, now, always. We're still in a moment of crisis. It just doesn't look that way on the surface. But it's those churches, and those leaders, who know it, and rise to it, that flourish.

This past December, my son and I visited Yad Vashem, the Holocaust museum in Jerusalem. That museum is a long zigzagging tunnel filled with grim relics that document a dark and violent history. But near the end of the tunnel is one room of hope. It tells the story of various acts of defiance and heroism, of those who risked their lives to save Jewish people. Prominent among the memorials is a tribute to La Chambon, and its church, and Andre Trocme, its pastor. We were deeply moved to visit the place.

But I find myself more and more praying for more churches and leaders like that, here, now, always.

Flourishing. Really?

James Watson, Corps Health and Planting Consultant, The Salvation Army Canada and Bermuda

I had the privilege of hosting the Flourishing Congregations research team in Kitchener in late June and I genuinely enjoyed the experience. Excellent to see people on the front lines and some of us who serve as coordinators interacting on the questions of what makes congregations flourish.

I did struggle with the five headings of the traits. I found that if I (strategically) covered the descriptions, I could see in the headings characteristics I have identified in congregations which have failed to flourish (either temporarily or permanently). Here would be my concerns about the five traits based on over a decade of being an interdenominational observer of Canadian congregational life:

Clear Self Identity – Some of the congregations I have connected with could articulate who their individual members were, valued traditions of their church and some goals or mission or vision statements, but were also clearly failing to flourish. They knew who they were, they were often happy to be who they were, but they were aging and dwindling.

Committed Leadership – A few congregations had very committed leadership ... to the extent that they did not realize they were blocking others from opportunities to lead. Some churches have watched generational cohorts of young leaders leave for other opportunities and have not recognized that they actually discouraged involvement (... so they could experience control or hold onto their leadership title or resist new cultural expressions of worship or were impatient in the ability of others to grow into a role, etc.).

Desire to Grow – It is very common to encounter struggling groups who strongly express their desire to grow. At some point in the downward spiral it becomes a survival instinct. The more difficult tests come when they try to imagine what they would change in order to develop in new ways, actually make changes (or not) and evaluate whether their ideas put into action contributed to growth (...or what kind of growth they actually experienced).

Hospitable Community – Unless there is ongoing conflict, most church groups can describe the ways in which their community is hospitable. When you talk to the people who are still part of the congregation (as opposed to those who have already left or those who have not yet visited), they can usually give reasons why they stick around. The key question is: Hospitable to whom? Do they have a "holy huddle" or have they learned how to make "outsiders" feel welcome?

Vibrant Spiritual Life – This all hinges on how we define "vibrant." It is not unusual for struggling congregations to feel comfortable with their current spiritual practices (although there may be mixed feelings). How can we identify the ways we can take risks that stretch our faith and identify the Holy Spirit at work in our midst and our surrounding community?

For those of you who have read the descriptions of the five traits, it is obvious that my ability to harpoon the traits is nullified by many of the details already used to define the traits. I suspect clarification of these definitions will be one of the big "wins" in doing research into flourishing, Canadian congregations over the next three years. The more carefully we can reflect on the "angel" of our congregation (Revelation 2-3), the greater success we will have identifying new ways that God may be opening up for us to flourish.

Thinking One Can: Believing Your Congregation Can Flourish

Dr. Peter Coutts, Author of *Choosing Change: How to Motivate Churches to Face the Future*

Do you remember the children's book *The Little Engine that Could*? The story was first published over 100 years ago in a curriculum for Sunday school children. It was re-published in 1905 under the title *Thinking One Can*.

I think every flourishing congregation travels the flourishing path with the little tank engine's attitude: "we think we can!" One cannot overstate the importance of capability beliefs when it comes to congregational motivation to pursue its vision for the future. Here's what psychology knows about the sources of motivation for change:

- 10% of motivation comes from recognizing that a gap exists between how things are now and how people want things to be

- 20% of motivation comes from committing to an intention to deal with the gap
- 70% of motivation comes from the belief that you are able to do what you intend to do

Many congregations get stuck at the discrepancy gap, overwhelmed by their sense of what needs to be done. Like the engines in the children's story looking at the load that must be hauled up the hill they say "that's too much pull for me." In fact, a congregation may have come by this belief honestly from their experience. It may have tried—and failed—a few times to bring about desired change. This can lead to a condition psychologist Martin Seligman called "learned helplessness": the belief that the congregation is unable to deal with the gap between how things are now and how people want things to be. Learned helplessness diminishes hope.

But learned helplessness is a belief. Conversely, thinking one can is a belief. So how do you help a congregation shift from one belief to the other and embark on the path to flourishing? Here are three proven strategies to strengthen a congregation's capability beliefs.

Strategy #1: Persuasion: Learn to tell the stories of congregational life in a way that helps congregants come to appreciate that they are able. "Remember when we set our minds to do X (whatever it was)? That was a big goal but we did it! We've shown ourselves that we can rise to the challenge …" As faith communities we also affirm that God helps the people of God. Like Paul can we come to believe "I can do all things through God who strengthens me" and "If God is for us then who can stand against us?"

Strategy #2: Help Congregants to Prove Themselves Wrong: Help congregants adopt a series of achievable goals and to attain those goals. Choose challenges that will require the congregation to step up, but not have to step too far up. The leadership goal here is to help the congregation learn through its experience that it is not helpless. When the congregation reflects on its successful experiences of attaining its goals, overcoming obstacles, and persevering until the conclusion, the experience can strengthen congregants' capability beliefs. It can help congregants to say, "so maybe we can tackle a bigger hill next!"

Strategy #3: Look for the Little Engines that Could (And Did!): The traditional telling of The Little Engine that Could ends too soon with the little tank engine rolling down the far side of the hill puffing confidently "I thought I could! I thought I could!" The story should have one additional paragraph pointing back to the engines in the yard who thought "that's too much pull for me." What do you suppose these larger engines would think after seeing the little tank engine succeed? They probably thought, "well, if that little engine could do it, then I can do it!" Help congregants observe, learn from and draw confidence from the experience of others who did what you want to do. Look for congregations who once looked like your congregation and made the change your congregation wants to make. Sure: learn how they did it—that helps. But more importantly help congregants believe that if that congregation (or better yet, those congregations) could do it, then our congregation can do it.

Every flourishing congregation started with the belief that it was able and their journey is sustained by the same belief. Believing we are able—through God's strength and by the unique giftedness of the congregation—fosters hope . . . and that hope can help the congregation climb its next hill.

The Safest Place in the World

Dr. Syd Hielema, Team Leader for Faith Formation Ministries for the Christian Reformed Church

Some years ago a friend told me that he had asked his 16 year old daughter what she considered to be the safest place in the world. She pondered this question for a few moments, and then replied, "it would have to be last month at our annual congregational retreat, when we ended by forming a large circle, holding hands, and singing "Bind us Together" acapella.

I had been part of that same circle, so I spent quite a bit of time pondering her response. What was it about our congregation that led her to make this powerfully moving declaration?

As I pondered, I realized that she was describing our congregational culture. It was as if she said, "there's something about our congregational culture that makes me feel very safe" (though I'm sure she had never heard that phrase before). Congregational culture refers to that hard-to-define reality which embodies the way folks experience a congregation, and she named her experience.

Culture is hard to define, but it's comprised of practices that are concrete and observable. So, I asked myself, "what practices has she been part of that have shaped her way of experiencing the congregation?" and this list came to my mind: Every Sunday she heard us share prayer requests prior to the congregational prayer, and as she listened, she learned that believers of all ages had joys and struggles and were willing to be publicly vulnerable with one another. Every Sunday she heard preaching that pointed to the gracious heart of God, preaching that was shaped by sturdy theology, illuminating stories and lovely humor, a combination that helped to engage her on a deep level.

She was a good musician, and the church provided opportunities for her to sing as part of an intergenerational worship team, and to regularly play her clarinet as part of an accompaniment ensemble. She had regular opportunities to exercise specific leadership gifts in areas such as writing for the congregation's newsletter and teaching Sunday School.

The annual retreat itself was a congregational practice that her family never missed, and somehow it served to consolidate and focus all the other practices. I could add more to the list, but you get the idea. She participated in a set of congregational practices that, when experienced together, shaped a congregational culture that felt to her like the safest place in the world.

I'm continuing to ponder my friend's daughter's comment, because two of my deepest longings are that (1) thousands of believers of all ages would say similar things about their congregations, and that (2) Faith Formation Ministries -- along with several other CRCNA partners -- would continue to support congregations in forming such places.

Why does this matter?

Paul declares that our congregations are temples, places where God himself lives! There's a direct connection between the way we experience our congregations and the way in which we come to know God. "The Lord is my rock, my fortress and my deliverer; my God is my rock, in whom I take refuge, my shield and the horn of my salvation, my stronghold" (Ps. 18: 2). In other words: the safest place in the world.

Originally posted April 14 on the Network at:
http://network.crcna.org/faith-nurture/safest-place-world

Your Church Needs More Charisma. And Maybe Less.

Dr. Peter Schuurman, Adjunct Professor, Redeemer University College

My research has been in the area of mega-church leadership, and I have heard two common remarks about the charismatic leader. From congregations searching for a pastor, comes this wish: "If we could just find a dynamic, charismatic leader, our church would surely flourish!" Coming from the opposite assessment of charisma, is this critique of mega-churches: "They may have a charismatic leader, but what will the congregation do when he or she abuses their power, or gets hit by a bus?"

Both remarks betray a misunderstanding about the nature of charisma, and by breaking down the term into three contrasting meanings, we can better discern the role charisma might play in congregations and their flourishing. Charisma is not a quick fix for a shrinking congregation, but neither is it necessarily a dangerous liability.

The first meaning of charisma is a spiritual meaning—something many Christians actually forget. St. Paul used the Greek term meaning "gift of grace" to emphasize the democratic nature of the church: he said that every believer has charisma—the Holy Spirit generating some gift for service in their life (see for example 1 Cor. 12:1-11). Leadership here is just one of many, many gifts of the Spirit, including showing mercy, serving, giving, administration, and speaking in tongues and their interpretation. These gifts, if not confounded by organizational bureaucracy but nurtured by spiritual disciplines and theological virtues, work together to create a vibrant community of faith and service.

In this sense, your church always can use more charisma. We should all be charismatic Christians to some degree.

Secondly, the most common meaning of charisma today is a situational meaning, arising out of the work of sociologist Max Weber one hundred years ago. He explained that in a context of tired traditions and bureaucratic boredom, where anxieties and uncertainties are intensifying, an exceptional leader may arise who is perceived to have a message and mission that offers hope and a future. Followers are totally devoted to this visionary leader and tell stories of his or her greatness. Think of Churchill during World War II or Barack Obama or Justin Trudeau after their uncharismatic predecessors. My research was on the popular Pastor Bruxy Cavey and The Meeting House, and their "irreligious" approach to church in secular Canada. Unlike Paul's spiritual charisma, this charisma arises as a relationship between a leader and their followers in a particular situation. It suggests heroism as much as servanthood, and unless its properly stewarded, may fizzle out or even go awry.

Your church may not need this kind of charisma as much as you think. Or maybe it's needed in a small dose. Still, we know that leadership is also a spiritual gift, and historical examples like Moses, Martin Luther, Charles Spurgeon and Billy Graham abound—charismatic leaders whose legacy displays a fruitfulness that last for ages.

Finally, there is one other, more critical understanding of the word charisma: charisma as a contrived popular image. I build off historian Daniel Boorstin's book *The Image: A Guide to Pseudo-Events in America* (1961) to explain how a form of charisma can be manufactured through management, marketing, and metrics. Rather than the charisma of a hero, this is the charisma of the celebrity, whom Boorstin defines as "a person who is known for his well-knownness." Contrived charisma arises from calculated use of mass media and social media, and is often associated with gimmicks, glamour or spectacle. Many lay people have come to expect this promotional approach today—unless they are wary and cynical about such artifice.

To a degree, in our internet age celebrated pastors cannot avoid this additional gloss of contrived charisma. It comes with having one's image on a screen—on TV, on a computer, or on a jumbotron. Congregations need to be wary of desiring this kind of charismatic glow, for it promises more than it delivers, and can fade very quickly. Moreover, it can become a trap, a gilded cage difficult to break out of—both for the branded pastor and congregation.

Three Notions of Charisma

Type	Charisma$_1$	Charisma$_2$	Charisma$_3$
Description	*spiritual*	*situational*	*contrived*
Author	St. Paul	Max Weber	Daniel Boorstin
Source	gift of grace/God	confluence of social factors	media and marketing
Embodiment	church community	heroic leader	celebrities
Meaning	a diversity of talents	revolutionary leadership	manufactured fame

In summary, there are three different meanings of charisma—spiritual, situational, and contrived. There is no doubt your congregation needs more spiritual charisma—the gift of grace displayed in the manifold blessings of the Holy Spirit to all believers. Your congregation may or may not need a charismatic leader perceived to have exceptional talent and a timely message; however, we know the Holy Spirit does gift certain leaders for particular situations. Finally, I suspect your congregation does not need to manufacture the superficial charisma of a mediated image that meets the cultural expectations of the average North American. Besides, many today are suspicious of a charismatic image, and only a truly Spirit-led charisma will lead to sustainable flourishing. At their core, what congregations really need is to follow one charismatic leader, and that's Jesus. By enacting his teaching and story, the Spirit's power will flow and grow a community of gifted leaders.

Ebb and Flow Decision Making

Sam Breakey, Church Health Strategist, Canadian Baptists of Western Canada

Congregations within our Baptist family lean towards one of two poles while making decisions. Some elect leaders to give spiritual leadership but then reserve the right of veto through grumbling and mistrust. Others, sit back and abdicate decision making to those in the back room. In each case, outcome ownership is limited.

Scripture teaches both the principle of spiritual eldership and the principle of the priesthood of believers. Healthy congregations practice both, rhythmically. Like tides that ebb and flow along a shoreline, congregational decision making that honours the authority of spiritual leaders as well as the insight and confirmation of the wider spiritual family, will instigate decision ownership and unity: The greater the issue, the greater will be the impact of honouring both principles.

For example, the leaders of one congregation I worked alongside were challenged to address significant repairs to a large parking lot that resulted primarily from not adding a second layer of pavement some fifteen years earlier. The deterioration of the surface significantly impacted the base, compounding the cost of repair. As always, other issues came into play – a pattern of investing in programs over infrastructure, the reduction of income following the departure of a previous lead pastor, a sizable property debenture, and a lack of transparency in decision making.

The leaders took the matter before the Lord, felt led to share the dilemma with the congregation, sought the permission at a congregational meeting to obtain three quotes, hesitantly took the results back to the congregation, invited wide feedback, then went back to develop a plan to raise funds for the repairs, then agreed only to sign a contract after a base amount was donated or pledged by the congregation. When the vote was eventually taken, the informed proposal received 100% approval and all the funds were received in full before the date of the final payment. Lessons learned from this process lead the leaders of this church to apply the ebb and flow pattern to further significant decisions. Unity and generosity soared as the leaders and congregation submitted the legitimate challenge to the Lord and to each other.

The bottom line: the authority of spiritual leadership is authenticated by attentiveness to the will of God and the needs of the people served.

Getting Children's Ministry Out of the Basement

Milissa Ewing, Pastor of Family Ministries at Tenth Church, Vancouver

"I wouldn't touch that job with a ten foot pole..." I said that. Not only once, but repeatedly when I was approached by Tenth Church to consider applying for the Pastor of Family Ministries position. Why would I willingly take on a job that exposes me to the constant criticism of parents, the chronic lack of committed volunteers, the professional status of an intern, all for the fraction of the salary that I made in my old job?

You have probably guessed the outcome: God did a little arm-twisting and I find myself in that very position that was so unappealing and I love my job. I have discovered that children's ministry is not the problem; the reputation of children's ministry is the problem.

Despite a recent survey in which the largest churches in Canada report that their growth is fueled by a strong children's and youth ministry (http://leadnet.org/canada/), the biggest barrier to recruiting passionate, talented staff and volunteers is perception: at its best children's ministry is a dry and dusty Sunday school lesson taught to a group of disinterested kids. At its worst, it's glorified babysitting in the church basement—while the "real" ministry happens upstairs.

I am convinced that one of the best things we can do to develop a flourishing children's ministry—and in turn a flourishing church—is getting children's ministries out of the basement. Think about your home. What usually ends up in the basement? The old couch. Moldy boxes of seasonal décor. Unused gym equipment. We send things down to the basement that we have no use for. Who wants to spend time in a dingy, dark basement?

Like many other churches, on Sundays our kids are in the literal church basement and we don't have the option of changing the physical location. However, we can change the symbolic location: when we commit to getting our kids out of the figurative church basement, we began to notice that the basement starts looking like a pretty appealing place to hang out.

People start volunteering. Volunteers become staff. Staff members are committed to being the best Children's Pastors they can be. And voila: children's ministry begins to thrive and grow.

Here at Tenth Church, we have made very intentional choices to change the common view of children's ministries: We launched a church initiative, "Fullness of Life for Every Child," flavored by sermons on the Biblical views of children (http://www.tenth.ca/series/fullness-of-life-for-every-child) and follow-up pledge cards, inviting congregants to commit their time or tithes to an organization that betters the life of a child. The Chair of our Board volunteers in the toddler room. Our senior leadership attends our volunteer appreciation events. The kids create top-notch art that adorns the sanctuary walls and they frequently participate in the service through music, prayer, and Scripture reading.

Essentially, we are giving children's ministry a public platform: taking what has always been there, hiding in the basement, and raising it up to its rightful place. We've given the kids a seat at the adult table.

This isn't a crass church-growth tactic: "improve children's ministry and see your church grow!" No. This reflects a biblically-based view of children in the church. Among many other references to children in the Bible, we see that leading children is the responsibility of the whole church (Deut. 6:4-7), that the kingdom of God belongs to children (Matt. 19:14), and that children lead us into worship (Matt 21:16).

So our quest to elevate children's ministry is not only necessary but right. After a few years of getting our children's ministry out of the basement, we are seeing results, not just in children's ministry, but in the church as a whole. As our volunteer base has doubled and the volunteers themselves are more passionate and excited about kids, parents are reporting that they are becoming more frequent attenders—because their kids love coming to church!

Transforming your Church

Dr. Clint Mix, Executive Pastor, Foothills Alliance Church, Calgary

Don't become so well-adjusted to your culture that you fit into it without even thinking. Instead, fix your attention on God (be transforming). You'll be changed from the inside out. (Romans 12:2, The Message)

In the classic movie, *The Wizard of Oz*, a sweet (albeit naïve) Dorothy experiences a tornado of change and all she knows is where she isn't... Kansas!

The Canadian culture and church have gone through a tornado of change and sometimes all we know is where we are not... "Kansas" (Christian Canada). Unlike Dorothy, we don't have a yellow brick road to follow to solve all our problems and get us back to "Kansas."

A side-note here ... it would definitely not be a presupposition of this article that the goal is to get back to Christian Canada, and frankly I doubt that Canada was ever Christian!

So how do churches respond to the challenges that so many face today? In recent decades, prophetic voices have been calling the church back to its mandate of participating with God in his mission of redeeming and reconciling "all things" (see Colossians 1:15-20).

Charles Ringma makes this poignant observation and reframing: "The missional church vision is not a programmatic response to the crisis of relevance, purpose and identity that the church in the Western World is facing, but a recapturing of biblical views of the Church all too frequently abandoned, ignored, or obscured through long periods of church history. It is a renewed theological vision of the church in mission, which redefines the nature, the mission and the organization of the local church around Jesus' proclamation of the good news of the Kingdom. Missional churches seek to respond to God's invitation to join Him in His mission in and for the world, as a sign, a servant and a foretaste of His Kingdom."

There are many ways that the church has become well-adjusted to our culture, and if we are to effectively participate with God (become flourishing), we need to be transforming away from these areas towards Kingdom values and practices.

From Consumerism to Cause: Church should no longer be about placating the wants of religious consumers and move towards empowering Christians to participate with God in his redemptive work.

From Counting to Kingdom: While people and money can be positive indicators of effective mission, when we make attendance and increased giving our goal (our marker of "flourishing") we make radically different decisions than if we make Kingdom impact on culture our goal.

From Determining to Discerning: A subtle way many churches have imbibed in our culture's values is by how we plan…most churches offer a perfunctory prayer and then determine their mission, values and objectives. If we (as we should!) believe that God is active in our churches and our world, then we move to a posture of discerning what he is doing in us, our communities and our global communities and participate with him.

To transform from determining our plans to discerning and participating with God's mission, many churches have invested a period of time in a communal discernment process of "Looking." This process includes discerning workshops, sermons, small groups and the individual practice of *lectio divina*. Throughout the discernment process churches are asking the question: "I wonder if God is saying that we could participate with him by …" Each posture of discerning includes elements of listening, prayer, biblical and theological reflection, cultural awareness and exegesis and other practices of discernment.

- **Looking Up:** Letting the nature and activity of God shape who we are and how we live
- **Looking Around:** Moving into the neighborhood (John 1:1, 14) to see what God is doing
- **Looking Back:** Leveraging God's past work to shape his present and future work (Habakkuk 3:2)

- **Looking In:** Becoming internally strong to empower your external focus. Becoming that sign of God's Kingdom on earth (Ephesians 5:25-33)
- **Looking Forward:** Moving from a posture of discernment to participation. Discerning and articulating God's calling, culture (values) and foci for fruitful participation with God in mission.

We may not have a yellow brick road, but we do know that God is faithful, and it's when we transform away from the values of culture and live into Kingdom values and practices that our churches can indeed be flourishing!

Why Your Congregation Needs a "Mind-altering" Experience

Dr. Cam Harder, Professor of Systematic Theology, Lutheran Theological Seminary, Saskatoon

I've spent 35 years as parish pastor and seminary professor looking for the secret to congregational vitality. I've tinkered with various in-vogue tools for enlivening worship, attracting youth, engaging the community, caring for each other, and so on. And most have had some benefit. But for me, real congregational change has usually happened after a mind-altering experience.

One of these took place at a parish I served in Calgary. My colleague brought in a group of lay people who, over a weekend of food and fun, shared stories of what God was up to in their lives. Then they asked us to break into groups and do the same. Now we were a pretty staid German bunch so most were a bit shocked. But hesitantly one after another began to say things like "well, I was able to make contact with our estranged daughter this week—I think that was God's doing." Or "I felt God's presence in our garden."

As we heard others saying they saw God in the ordinary stuff of their lives we began to wonder if perhaps the Creator of the Universe was active in our own humdrum lives. It was exciting, mind-altering! Over the next few weeks we had dozens of folks who asked if they could join (or start) a discipleship group.

When Jesus started his ministry, Mark says he went around shouting "Change your minds! See--God's reign is right here, close at hand!" Jesus helped people to see the world differently, to see it saturated by the gracious presence of an everywhere God.

There are a couple of approaches to ministry that I like to use to lead congregations into a mind-altering experience ("metanoia" for biblical scholars). The first changes the way we tell stories. The second shifts how we do accounting.

First the story-telling: All congregations tell Bible stories. Those stories give us a sense of God's "life-style," God's priorities and purposes. But we sometimes forget to ask "now where do you think you might have seen an expression of that Divine lifestyle, those priorities and purposes in your own life this week? Or in your congregation, or community?"

Noticing and naming God's current activity is surely one of the Church's key responsibilities. Yet our coffee conversation often seems focused (with painful precision) on the ways in which sin and chaos are ravaging our world. Certainly there is evil and suffering around us—and our media are only too happy to lay all the world's pain (far more than we can handle) at our doorstep. However the energy to invest in others' suffering, and the hope that we can make a difference, comes from seeing what God is doing around us to foster love, to build webs of shared lives, to sustain the struggling. It's "awe-some" to discover that God is doing far more than we realized. It's a joyful surprise to see that those things of which we despair (including ourselves) are actually the arena of God's life-giving work. And seeing what God is up to gives us hope-filled direction for ministry.

Then the accounting: Most congregations have been trained to track resources for ministry primarily in terms of money, buildings and clergy. But churches all over the world flourish without paid pastors and holy bricks. So sometimes it's best to mentally block out the "big three."

Out of their shadow the ministry world looks very different. We discover our congregation and community are a treasure trove of practical skills, personality gifts, wisdom gained from scars, natural resources, things folks would lend or give, creative interests and abilities. In fact, every congregation is rich, beyond measure. If they had eyes to see it none would close for lack of resources. It is mind-altering to discover the scope of the wealth God has given them, and exciting to creatively connect those resources for ministry.

My mind was altered when I came across these approaches in community development seminars. It's called "appreciative inquiry" when we focus our communal story-telling not on our problems but on what is working (theologically, on what God is up to). It's called "asset-mapping" when we track and mobilize the full resources of a community (God's gracious gifts). Never thought I'd find core tools for vital ministry outside the church. But apparently God is at work there too! What other mind-blowing discoveries might the Church make if it looked a bit farther afield?

Four Things To Know About The People Walking Through Your Church Doors

Darryl McAuley, Lead Pastor at McDiarmid Drive Alliance Church, Brandon

When I think of what it means to be a flourishing congregation, many images flood my mind. I think of a church that is growing, praying, on mission, united, and on the list goes.

The one aspect of being a flourishing church that has kept me intrigued over the past few months however, is how a flourishing congregation welcomes people to be part of their faith community. I am not talking about how a church transitions Christians disgruntled with their former church into new (down the block) pews/theatre seats/stacking chairs or whatever the church has chosen as their preferred seating option. I am talking about how flourishing congregations receive people who are exploring the very core and meaning of their life; their spiritual longings to know and be known by God.

I was recently part of a research project that studied churches in North America that were effective in transitioning the previously unchurched toward faith and church community life. As I spent time researching these churches there were a few common themes that surfaced. It seemed like when I talked to people who had recently transitioned into the Christian faith and community life, there were notable commonalities and shared experiences. Here are four things you should know about the people who are walking into your church for the first time:

They Are Afraid: If you ever wondered what the unchurched person is thinking as they drive onto your church property and pull open the door to your sacred space, you can summarize their emotions in one word, fear. People are terrified as they come through your doors. Church, as most of us realize, is one of the scariest places to enter. Although the unchurched may articulate it in different ways, they wonder if the people in the faith community will accept them.

They Are Navigating Major Life Experiences: People who are reaching out to the church are often reaching out because they are in the midst of a major life experience or transition. Relational stress, financial uncertainty, depression, addictions are but a few of the life experiences people are facing that push them toward reaching out to the church. They want help and the church is one of the places they reach out to for that help.

They Have A Longing To Fill the Empty Part of Their Soul: I recently sat with a group of people who had recently accepted Christ as their Savior. As each of them shared their stories of coming to faith, they all identified with each other's declaration that there was something missing in their souls. Although they didn't use the term, "God shaped vacuum," they did describe it in a similar fashion.

They Have Already Had Christians Influence Them: As I have talked with people who were previously unchurched I was surprised as I talked with them about people in their lives who have connected them to the Christian faith. It seems like there is always a praying grandmother, aunt, or father who has shared spiritual truths of the Christian faith. When they step into your facility, it probably won't be their first time at the rodeo and it should remind us of Paul's words, "I planted the seed, Apollos watered it, but God has been making it grow" (1 Corinthians 3:6 NIV).

The insights I have gained from studying the previously unchurched has changed the way I think of first time visitors to our church services. When I reach out and shake their hand for the first time, I think about what has brought them to our community of faith. I know they didn't "just show up," I know they have a story. By listening to peoples' stories, it has helped shaped the way I see our front door ministries but, more importantly, it has shown me how to reach out and love those who are searching to find meaning and hope in their life.

The Attributes of Strong Leadership & Tilling the Soil

John Pentland, Hillhurst United Church, Calgary
(www.hillhurstunitedchurch.com)

Jim Collins writes that it's not just good leadership that moves organizations or communities toward excellence, but "Level Five leadership creates the shift." According to Collins, the two primary attributes "Level Five" leaders possess are professional will, and personal humility.

By professional will, Collins is referring to both the vision a leader has of where the organization is going, and the passion to make that vision come to life. Level Five leaders hold an outward view, always considering what, creatively, is possible. In Christian terms, I see this as reflective of all the times Jesus provides yet another parable or yet another story or saying that sparks yet another way of thinking, living, being—while holding the Kingdom vision steady. The vision Jesus gave us was far beyond what a conflict-bound community could imagine: the call to greatness was articulated when he asked us to love each other. For the sake of extending the metaphor here, his so-called "professional will" could be seen in his relentless call to this loving vision, his speaking it, and his living it. As for "personal humility", this kind of integration of see-walk-talk is one way of understanding humility. Something greater than us is at play, and we are its servants. Of this Jesus is the Master. It feels a little strange to place a secular paradigm such as "professional will" and "personal humility" on the ministry of Jesus, but I press on because I propose that it shouldn't. Our world is not two worlds. Vision together with a will devoted to following where that vision might lead is an unstoppable combination.

People were drawn to Jesus—to the vision he held out for those who could see and hear, to what he said and how he said it, and to how he moved in the world. One of the primary ways he did all this was to seek to meet people where they were at, engage them, which he often did through inspired questions—he poses about 135 questions in the gospels. Asking sincere questions can be another way to define "humility"—make it a kind of freedom. For one, asking questions takes us out of the "having answers" mode. For another, it invites us to consider things from perspectives other than our own. And, for another, if we're interested in finding the right questions, then we let go of our agendas if even for a moment, and learn something. I feel Jesus posed his questions in order to discover, dream, imagine, better understand those around him, as much as to help those around him discover for themselves the spiritual life individually, together, and with God. In this way, charismatic leadership and humility need not be mutually exclusive.

All of which is to say the first step to strong leadership is asking questions and listening for, and to, the answers. Change comes into focus when we find and pose the right questions, and we can learn to do this. It is, for me, a spiritual practice. As one small support of this practice, I receive a leadership newsletter from consultant Corey Olynik that always includes a leadership "question" to work with. Here are five (random) examples:

- What words do you use when you describe your organization?
- Do you live your stories out loud?
- What is "so bad" in your organization, that you can laugh about?
- How has your mind changed in the last decade or two?
- Is your strategic vision a noun or a verb? Is it static or active?

Of course, there are endless questions, and not all questions are created equal. Even if Corey's questions aren't relevant to my own circumstance, at the very least this weekly email reminds me of the power of questioning and listening. A wonderful proposition to explore is how questions and answers exist in light of each other. The Einstein quote cited earlier which says that insanity is doing the same thing over and over and expecting different results suggests this relationship also. This means that we should not only be consciously asking questions, but aware of the nature, tone and content of the questions we're asking!

As many of the leadership experts suggest, questions, not answers, are the cornerstone leadership skill, and learning to ask the right question at the right time is an art. The power of asking questions causes the creative process to kick into gear. It gives people the opportunity to make a wholehearted investment, and if change is afoot, to take ownership. As we'll discuss later, this latter engagement with the process is, at root, what leadership most wants to inspire.

But answers DO have their place. Is a great church possible? Is it possible to make church something that matters, something that people love? With these and other questions held firmly in mind, the first year at Hillhurst was dedicated to doing a lot of listening. This is another primary leadership teaching. As much as we need to ask the right questions, equally important—and sometimes more difficult—we need to listen to the answers that come as well. Collins tells the story of when, as a first-year faculty member at Stanford, he sought out Professor John Gardner's guidance on how he might be a better teacher. Collins writes:

> Gardner, former Secretary of Health, Education and Welfare, founder of Common Cause, and author of the classic text Self-Renewal, stung me with a comment that changed my life. He said, 'It occurs to me, Jim, that you spend too much time trying to be interesting. Why don't you invest more time being interested.

And I was genuinely interested. I was interested in discovering who was in this congregation. That first year was spent questioning my way into the community, and listening toward where this group of people might want to go. There was a lot of watching and observing too—all of which was intended as a way to see what really mattered to folks in the pews. I was looking at what stirred people, moved them, and made their eyes glaze over.

I wondered what they were curious about. I wanted to know what inspired them—what ideas, what social justice work, what spiritual questions. I was also interested in discovering who had leadership skills and aspirations, who was willing to take risks, who were the pillars, who was willing to leave the past behind, who was full of creative ideas. Listening—being genuinely interested—like questioning is a way to embody humility.

And so is learning to wait, to be patient, not to rush things as the process unfolds. Attending to the timing of things and being sensitive to when the moment is ripe is another. Inviting possibility and accepting that it might be a false lead is another. Taking the time to be self-aware is yet another—and a very important—way to practice humility. Just like there's no room for complacency in the pews, there's absolutely no room for complacency here either.

I think of all this questioning and listening and waiting and watching as "tilling the soil." I have learned from personal experience and observation that leaders often get in trouble when they propose something without this kind of adequate tilling. The listening/observing/waiting time is key to being prepared. It should be noted that this tilling time wasn't a time of criticism for Hillhurst, but a time of optimism and increasing energy. And while I was not pushing a particular change agenda, I was actively seeking the people who wanted to help make the leap from here-to-there, whatever that change might turn out to be. I actively sought ways to allow people to step forward, have their voices heard, clarify their ideas, and be validated. I often used sermons as a means to report back to the community what people had expressed, telling a story of someone who yearned for more, or a person who actively responded to what was newly being offered.

This too is a kind of tilling the soil, preparing the creative field. Lifting up people around us, making the case for change by promoting new ways of thinking and being, inviting new voices to be heard—this is part of the work of a leadership aiming to facilitate positive shift—not force the change to happen. In this way, too, change is rightfully experienced as more organic, more responsive to what is needed, more integral—as indeed it is. All this is another way of looking at the quality of "humility."

Part of Hillhurst's mandate for me was "to connect with the wider community," so I took the questioning "out there" as well. Jesus was always inviting people to be inclusive. So we raised questions about who was already among us, and who was not there? What did we need to do to make people in the community feel comfortable about coming into our sanctuary? We worked to expand our understanding about street people and how they are as much the "Christ Amongst Us" as anyone. We undertook a lengthy conversation about LGBT folks and what it might be like for them to find a truly safe place to believe, to worship and to feel at home. We asked ourselves questions about how we might expand the compassionate ethic of Jesus to folks down the street at the coffee shops and stores: So much listening, so much observing, so many questions. This amounts to tilling the soil. It is seeking our vision and faithful spirit—the vision that will constitute our "professional will."

Again: leadership is the church's biggest challenge and greatest opportunity. As Collins points out, the business model isn't entirely suitable for church organization, but foundational leadership principles are—like listening, observing, validating, and being open to what comes, without imposing. On closer inspection, these principles are not really so far from our pastoral directives and traditional spiritual values.

The Church in Exile

Dr. Lee Beach, Associate Professor of Christian Ministry, McMaster Divinity College

The experience of living in a Post-Christian culture is settling in as a reality for the contemporary North American church. The ongoing move to the margins can leave Christians feeling discouraged and even doubtful about where God is in this time of exilic experience. Why would God allow this to happen? Why does God not show his power more clearly in a time like this? How are we supposed to move forward in a time when the Christian message is losing traction in an increasingly secular culture? These are all questions and that one should not feel guilty for asking.

The experience of cultural displacement is not new for the people of God. Ancient Israel experienced a similar displacement when they were conquered by the Babylonians, in the early part of the 6th Century BCE. For them living in Babylonian captivity brought about questions of God's sovereignty and faithfulness. If one reads the biblical book of Lamentations and the exilic Psalms (44,

74, 79, 89, 102, 106 and 137) it is easy to spot the fact that Israel did not find the experience of marginalization an easy one to embrace in light of their understanding of who God was and who they were as his people. These biblical texts reflect a "spirituality of exile" that may offer the contemporary Canadian church some insight into how to process our own cultural dislocation. These texts offer a way for church leaders to give spiritual direction to their congregations in a time of exile. The following four movements reflect the exilic wisdom of our ancestors in the faith.

Lament: The first response that Israel offered to God regarding their reality of being deported to the margins of Babylon was lament. Lament is the language that gives voice to the anguish of spiritual exile. It is the genre of prayer that expresses the incongruity of life experience with what one previously understood to be the character of God. The laments of the Hebrew Bible during the early exilic period were bold acts of discourse which reveal Israel's unwillingness to remain passive in the face of their plight. So too does the church in Canada today need to lament our situation by acknowledging the losses and challenges we face as well as our doubts and fears about the future. Church leaders must allow room in their congregations for this kind of conversation.

Memory: An important part of Israel's finding their way forward in a time of exile was their remembering how God had worked in the past, particularly in his delivering power for Israel from their internment in Egypt. The call to remember that God had been faithful in the past was a catalyst to Israel's belief that God would be faithful to them in their exilic context. Church leaders today must connect their congregations to these biblical narratives in a fresh way so that they may also be inspired by how God has worked in the past and be reminded that our exile is nothing new, nor is it in any way antithetical to the way that God works in the world. We are in good company and remembering the way that God has been present in the previous exilic experiences of his people forms a foundation for us to move forward.

Re-Orientation: In understanding their situation Israel had to come to terms with the fact that they had not been faithful in their covenant relationship with God and exile was the result. This required them to honestly define their reality and respond with repentance and a resolve to live differently. In a similar way leaders in the contemporary church need to help their churches understand what has changed and how those changes affect us. They need to help the church come to terms with the way the church may have contributed to its own demise and how we can repent from unhelpful attitudes and behaviours and respond effectively to our current circumstances.

Hope: The exilic prophets never ceased providing hope to Israel and reminding the people that they still had a central place to play in God's overarching plan for the world. They offered a hopeful vision for the future (Isaiah) and also directed some tangible initiatives that expressed faith in action (Nehemiah). Church leaders today must also cast a hopeful vision into the lives of their congregations and must also help them to determine ways that they can serve their communities constructively so that God's kingdom can grow in their specific context. The combination of keeping hope alive through good words and embodying the kingdom through good works is foundational to cultivating hope in the church today.

Forming an exilic spirituality in contemporary Canadian congregations is a key work of ministry leadership today. As we help develop the disciplines of an exilic spirituality in the life of our congregation we will offer the kind of spiritual direction to the local church that will help it flourish in Post-Christendom Canada.

The Flourishing Church in the New Testament and Today

April Yamasaki, Lead Pastor at Emmanuel Mennonite Church, Abbotsford

Several months ago, I was invited to speak to a group of pastors and other church leaders on spiritual renewal for congregations. They had been focusing a great deal on change—how to respond to changing culture, how to manage change within the church--- and I had been asked to shift the conversation from what to do about change to how we might find spiritual renewal in changing times. What does it mean to be a spiritually renewed church in the midst of change?

When the New Testament speaks of the church, it's remarkably free of our modern pre-occupation with statistics and demographics. We're never told the membership numbers for the church in Corinth, Rome, Thessalonika, or any of the early churches. The New Testament author mentions widows, but not how many, or if there were more women than men. Although Jesus welcomed parents and young children, we don't know how many young families were part of the church, or if there were many youth and young adults.

Instead of majoring on demographics and numbers, the New Testament describes the spiritually renewed church this way:

Let love be genuine; hate what is evil, hold fast to what is good; love one another with mutual affection; outdo one another in showing honor. Do not lag in zeal, be ardent in spirit, serve the Lord. Rejoice in hope, be patient in suffering, persevere in prayer. Contribute to the needs of the saints; extend hospitality to strangers.

Bless those who persecute you; bless and do not curse them. Rejoice with those who rejoice, weep with those who weep. Live in harmony with one another; do not be haughty, but associate with the lowly; do not claim to be wiser than you are. Do not repay anyone evil for evil, but take thought for what is noble in the sight of all. If it is possible, so far as it depends on you, live peaceably with all. (Romans 12:9-18)

That's the kind of flourishing church that I would want to belong to, that God calls us to, that I think people in our world are hungry for today. And while the Bible isn't exactly a how-to manual, I believe that Romans 12:1-2 tells us something about how to be flourishing, spiritually renewed churches today.

First of all, we can't get there on our own. The chapter begins with an appeal to readers "by the mercies of God." We can pray for spiritual renewal for our churches and for ourselves. We can explore different spiritual disciplines to help prepare the way. We can research, experiment, and apply various strategies. But we can't control spiritual renewal, or make it happen by our own efforts. Instead, spiritual renewal comes to us by the mercies of God.

At the same time, the text urges readers to present our bodies to God as our spiritual worship. If we're looking for renewal, we need to take seriously our whole selves—body, soul, and spirit. We are embodied souls, spiritual beings in the flesh. It's through our bodies that we express what we believe and feel and think. So spiritual renewal will involve concrete acts of love, worship, serving, giving, and so much more. It means showing up in the real world.

Spiritual renewal also means more than going through the motions. As we present our bodies, we are also urged "do not be conformed to this world, but be transformed by the renewing of your minds." To act differently means we will also need to think differently. While the world may say, get even, we are to think and practice patience and trust in God: Instead of pride, humility; instead of cursing, an offer of blessing; instead of hostility, practicing hospitality to strangers.

I appeal to you therefore, brothers and sisters, by the mercies of God, to present your bodies as a living sacrifice, holy and acceptable to God, which is your spiritual worship. Do not be conformed to this world, but be transformed by the renewing of your minds, so that you may discern what is the will of God—what is good and acceptable and perfect (Romans 12:1-2).

Church: Where Exactly Can It Flourish?

Matthew Fillier, B.A., M.Div, Ordained Minister, United Church of Canada

Are pews and steeples necessary for God's people?

In 2014, I was fortunate to be able to attend the Greenbelt festival in Cheltenham England, as part of a delegation of people under thirty five from the United Church of Canada. While I've since passed that young-ish threshold as established by my denomination, I will never forget the experience of faith I encountered there.

While Greenbelt is an annual gathering of thousands of people from around the world and has frequently taken place in the same location, it has moved from time to time. Can you imagine the logistical nightmare?

Have you ever changed the location of your Sunday morning worship service? What happened? Did the same twenty thousand people come from around the world?

Could everyone see, hear and sit comfortably? Could they find the coffee pot and the washroom? Did everyone clamour "Let's do this again next week!" or was the response a little more…muted? I think the response says a lot about a congregation's culture and identity.

Space matters when it comes to spirit. It has always been thus in the Christian tradition. Where we do what we do is buried deep in our ancestral bones. It imprints us with meaning and identity perhaps as much as prayer and praise. This truth rings true in Western Christianity as it seems definitively woven into the Canadian experience. When I think of how many church buildings have either disbanded (ceased to exist) or amalgamated in the Maritime Conference of my denomination, there's been far more of the former than the latter.

In my own pastoral charge (parish) during the late 1980's, two of the three congregations closed their buildings and attempted to knit their fishing nets together. It's a tricky business as Peter and Paul have shown us. Some twenty years afterward, I'm amazed at the people I still visit who identify solely with the former building and have ceased to "go to church" at all. For several of them, when the doors of a particular building closed, so did their witness in public worship.

We go to the movies. We go to the mall. We go for coffee. In the West we go for something in return, and thus we go to church and not just any church, but my church.

Place matters.

There's a reason our ancestors made the sign of the fish and met at particular times in particular places – they witnessed in a time when their faith could forfeit their lives. Sanctuary was a place of safety, whether it be a house or on a field or beside the lakeshore. Today these sanctuaries are a lot bigger, more expensive and difficult to maintain but they are imbued with baptisms, Christmas Eve pageants, funerals, weddings and countless other rites of religious passage that bind faith to a particular location and time. Place gives power to the romance of cultural and social nostalgia that binds a community together. No wonder our religious edifices can be at once both a stone around our neck and a foundation beneath our feet.

As mainline denominations struggle with an organization infrastructure designed for a bygone era, moving out from under the steeple isn't easy for God's people. The sign of resurrection is surely the empty tomb, but the gospel narratives are decidedly skimpy on the details of that rolling stone.

As the mainline church strives to emerge from the graveside of a fallen Christendom in a multicultural and diverse Canada, does place still have the same power to constitute a community of faith? Is our expression of Christianity so bound to buildings that we can't conceive of a religious life evolving beyond them? What if you could plant a church without a building? I'm not talking about meeting in a cinema or a high school gymnasium or a store-front church. I mean no particular place because it is possible in every place. Would such a community wither on the vine without the root of a foundation and steeple? Could it grow not just in a neighbourhood but an entire region? What if it didn't have a minister, an administrator, a board or a list of committees requiring an ecclesial translator to decipher the meaning and purpose of their jabberwocky acronym jargon?

That's one of the many questions I have for "Be.", an emerging ministry within the Maritime Conference of the United Church of Canada. It started from the experience of our regional annual meeting. It turns out that when you get people together in a hockey rink instead of a church building, God only knows what can ensue. Conga lines of singing, prayer circles of healing, a full piece worship band sharing music that spans the globe and not just a hymn-book – and the single largest gathering of youth in our church.

Place matters!

From that annual worship experience has sprung deep hunger pains for something that many, but not solely, our younger sisters and brothers in Christ were hankering for. After experiencing an inclusive culture with few borders of experimentation in worship and liturgy, how was it a colleague of mine put it? You can't put the rabbit back in the hole. What if you didn't have to worry about whether worship was "contemporary" or "traditional"? What if you didn't have to struggle about piano or organ? What if you didn't have to tussle with the worship committee about the merits of projection or whether contemporary music can easily be translated to quench the questing Christian's soul? All such conversations are surely important, but the opportunity to move beyond them is equally desirable for many leaders and searchers alike.

The easiest way to describe "Be." is that it's a verb instead of a noun. As an expression of church it isn't a particular building that comes to mind – it's possible all across Nova Scotia, New Brunswick, and PEI.

We held our events on Friday nights. It's amazing what happens when you're not bound to Sunday at 11am. Musicians who would never be able to play together, jammed. People gathered from vastly different pews that had never sat together, broke bread, shared stories of faith, and stood together. The guest speakers were not ministers, but everyday people struggling and giving thanks for their unique experience of faith and spirituality.

We plan to hold our events everywhere from corner coffee shops to farmer's markets to public squares. They take place every few months and feature food, worship, and deeper conversation than often seems challenging in the sixty minutes or less commandment of so much mainline Protestant worship. We planted leadership teams that advertised locally inside and outside our traditional communities of faith and watched to see what would sprout. The results of our first round of events were profound and inspiring. It was also not without a steep learning curve and many challenges. In my next post, I'll detail how the first event Halifax transpired and what we learned from it. In the meantime, take a second and visit www.be-maritimes.org to learn more. Can a community of people who share neither pew nor steeple flourish? I'm looking forward to finding out.

Confessions of a Church Drifter

Timothy Quek, Lead Pastor (English) at North Toronto Chinese Alliance Church

I sat at the table in Starbucks across from Tara. From the start, I knew I was not in a welcoming conversation when she refused to order anything though she had chosen the venue. So I dutifully got myself a coffee to legitimize our occupation of a space in this citadel of transient community.

Drifting as a Disastrous Pattern: Tara had come to our church from another about two years or so ago, seeking what she called "meaningful connections" among believers her age. She was in her mid to late 20s, seemingly interested in spiritual growth, and wanting to contribute to the body of believers at our location. A couple of red flags fluttered in my mind when she spoke about being from a Christian family that worshipped at yet another church, and a dating relationship that "ended rather poorly" at one other church in between, but she seemed genuine enough in her desire to come and to stay.

I wondered what those red flags were all about until that day at Starbucks. After all, every reason she offered for her journey down one aisle and up the other in the experience called church seemed plausible. So we embraced her in our community with open arms.

The result was devastating. For the two years that Tara was among us, we discipled her, loved her, helped her to discover her gifts, and gave her the co-leadership of one of our small groups. When she chose to leave, her small group went into turmoil and many drifted off to other churches or left church altogether. One drifter leads many to drift.

A community with members connected and committed to each other functions, in the Apostle Paul words, as a body. And when a body experiences a loss of a member, the grief and pain is often difficult to bear. Perhaps this is the reason many believing communities choose to remain somewhat aloof of new members till they've proven themselves over time.

Hello Goodbye: Some of the members of that community had asked me to talk to Tara to gain some perspective on why she'd chosen to leave. I wasn't quite prepared to at first because I'd been there before - spending energy on chasing down those who choose to leave instead of calling those who are lost. However, I agreed. And so this finds me in Starbucks.

Our conversation was awkward. Tara and I had spent much time over many coffees talking about life. But this conversation was about death. In an open posture of learning, I popped the question, "So why did you decide to leave?" She was immediately defensive, but we managed to grope around long enough to give me some valuable insights to my simple question.

1. Temporary Neighbours: "I've been here for two years," Tara said at one significant point in our conversation, "I think it's time for me to move on to fresh experiences." The thought was at first offensive, but upon thinking about it, it makes perfect sense. In a generation where upward career mobility is defined by two year commitments, and car leases, cellphone contracts and the like are best under that same time frame, we are likely to be shaped by a the culture of success that considers two years as the upper end of career or FOMO stagnation.

The work of bringing people to church and being attractive enough to have them stay at church is one that has set numerous good minds to work. Billy Hornsby in his book, *The Attractional Church*, cautions that the church today loses more people that it gains, and that as churches lean heavily on creating models to increase numbers, the inability to create a strong relational environment means that people who come form only a shallow sense of belonging to the local church.

Yet the culture of drifting from church to church persists beyond attractional models. It is the story of a corporate world gone awry, rewarding the creation of temporary neighbours in exchange for upward mobility. As a body of believers, it is necessary to address the prevailing culture of disconnectedness. Since the experience with Tara, I've taken the concept of community in Christ and made it a basis for a number of teaching platforms - sermons, studies, discussions - with the effect that the ship started to make its slow but definite turn.

2. Serial Drifting: In a moment of inspiration, I asked Tara about the other churches she'd said goodbye to. Remembering our conversation from when she first came, I was surprised by her answer. "I still have great friends in all of them," she piped, and cheerfully announced that she would continue to go to a small group at my church while exploring a different church.

I remember well Larry Osborne's beautiful illustration that the "stickiness" of a church (hence the title of his book Sticky Church) depends on the number and the degree of connectedness that a person has with a community. It brought a smile to my face to imagine what Osborne would say about this serial search for sticky communities without wanting to actually stick around.

I've learned since such conversations with the Taras of our church world to make an encouragement not to leave a church (to come to mine) a part of my initial conversation. If hurt, anger, disagreement, boredom, disconnectedness and blame populate our churches as a justification to drift from one community of worship to another, we will find ourselves full of edgy, disconnected people and a church system built on the newest gadgets to entertain a fluid crowd. I think the energies of the church are better used in Great Commission efforts - discipleship, evangelism, instruction, application, leadership development - rather than trying desperately to keep a drifting population.

3. Living Room Discipleship: As our conversation at Starbucks progressed, my sense that Tara's determination to drift would again go unaddressed by her next community of choice became an uneasy knot in my throat. I ventured a thought with her.

"If you understand a community of believers to be a family," I ventured, "do you think the family suffers when people decide to leave rather than stay to work at being a stronger family?" She drew back from the table, and I sensed that our conversation was nearing an end. "You're making me feel guilty," she declared. "It's a matter of fit. When I no longer sense a fit, I move on."

What immediately entered my mind were people in a house lounging in the living room. They're comfortable; they appear connected; they look perfectly happy with each other. But they're in a living room. After a good time of connection, they leave. They don't unpack and tuck in for the long haul. They're living room disciples.

Discipleship through the lens of Jesus looks quite different. From the dusty streets of Capernaum to the locked doors of the Upper Room, the disciples learned to hang together. Did a fisherman fit with a tax collector, or a Zealot with a doubter? I think we overrate the idea of fit when the call to discipleship is not to love who you are (which is the basis for the concept of "fit") but to love as Jesus loved. Loving who we are leads to the desire to hang out with people most like us. That leads to segregation, cliques, bigotry, and social exclusivism. As church, we do that by reflex when we let the children take their noise to the basement, and the "young people" their inattentiveness to the "youth service."

If indeed we are family, then living rooms need to progress to dining rooms, and dining rooms to bedrooms where truly connective discipleship takes place. Discipleship needs to be the intentional Great Commission activity it's meant to be, and it needs to take place within the body by more than ones considered the "super elite."

Come Home: As we got up to leave (I think she was ready before I was), I could feel the unsettled rush of caffeine grip me after consuming an extra large Americano without cream or sugar on an empty stomach at 8 in the evening. There are no words to describe the nauseating emptiness of trying to understand why people choose to drift from church to church. It weakens the body of Christ; it exhausts the faithful; it discourages the weak.

I remember recently picking up a book by Patricia Paddey and Karen Stiller called Shifting Stats Shaking the Church. One particularly poignant interview that they recorded was with a woman who had been a refugee, lost in the sea of Canadian society. In her drifting, she found church. I will thus leave the last word to her. "When I came to this church, I understood what I have hearing since I was a child - that the church is a family. The whole week I would be running around, dealing with [everything], and I would really feel like I was in a foreign country. But when I'd get to church, I felt like I was among family. I was home."

A Recipe for Church Growth

Dr. David Millard Haskell, Wilfrid Laurier University

Photo: Courtesy of Elmdon Church, Solihul, UK

As a boy in the 1970s, I often accompanied my grandmother to her neighborhood United Church for Sunday service. Back then my Grandma's church was packed with young and old alike. It wasn't unique. The other Mainline Protestant houses of worship in her town—the local Anglican, Lutheran, and Presbyterian churches—were all filled.

Times change. In Canada, the US and the UK the "Mainline" has moved to the "Sideline." My grandmother's United church was torn down just two years ago. Again, not unique. Mainline Protestant churches across the West are closing every month.

Curious about the root cause of this ongoing exodus of attendees, a few years ago some colleagues and I launched a study of Mainline Protestant churches. The main findings came out in academic journals end of November and early December, 2016, and were reported by the media.

To get to our findings we processed mounds of survey data comparing the traits of over 1000 attendees from a selection of growing Mainline Protestant churches—which were difficult to find—to a near equal number of attendees from declining Mainline Protestant churches. We also surveyed and interviewed the clergy who serve them. When we used statistical analysis to disentangle which factors are influencing growth, conservative Protestant theology was a significant predictor. Our research stands out because past studies have suggested theology and church growth are not linked. They are.

Like all researchers, my colleagues and I are pleased that our work is getting noticed by the public. However, our worry is that the public will seize on this single, albeit very important, finding from the study and miss some other noteworthy discoveries. For example, in addition to establishing that conservative Protestant doctrine predicts increase our analysis also showed that two other factors play a significant positive role in church growth: contemporary worship and emphasis on youth programming. Put simply, churches that adhere to conservative Protestant theology are more likely to grow than those that do not, but their chance of growth increases when they employ drums and guitars in service and connect with youth in multiple ways inside and outside the church.

I can imagine there may be church-goers of a more liberal theological persuasion who read the list of "ingredients" above and wonder: "Can my church just ignore that conservative theology piece but bring in a band for Sunday and start doing more events for kids during the week and expect our pews to fill with people?"

The good news is that with a strategy like that your church will likely attract more people; the bad news is that it probably won't keep them. Catchy music and engaging events for youth are enough to make some unaffiliated individuals want to go to your church. But, for a church to actually grow, the attendees must feel they need to go. For a host of reasons centering on their more literal interpretation of the Bible (which, among other things, commands them to love the Lord with all their heart, mind, and strength) churches adhering to conservative Protestant doctrine seem better at eliciting that response. In our published work we theorize that growing churches' tendency to use strategies like contemporary worship and clever youth events also rises out of conservative doctrine. When you literally believe it's your mission to "Go and make disciples" you find innovative means to reach that goal.

Unfortunately, there's more bad news for those looking for the miracle cure to an ailing church. While our study identifies the factors that predict growth—conservative theology, contemporary worship, and emphasis on youth programming—churches that have all three are not guaranteed growth. Certainly, they are better positioned for numerical increase than other churches without the three factors, but we can envision circumstances where even that's not enough. For example, churches with unfriendly congregations or terrible preachers would be unlikely to grow no matter what. Another article my colleagues and I just published in the Canadian Review of Sociology titled "Factors Influencing Church Choice" explores this phenomenon and makes that case.

My grandmother's church was a friendly, lively place. Before it joined the denomination of the United Church of Canada in 1925, it was an evangelical Methodist church and it still had that vibe.

Occasionally, during the services we attended together, the congregation would harken back to their Methodist roots and sing the Gospel song "Gimme that old time religion, it's good enough for me." For my grandmother and her fellow congregants, the "old time religion" may have been enough, but today, for church growth, it's just a start.

Dr. David Millard Haskell is author along with Drs. Kevin Flatt and Stephanie Burgoyne of "Theology Matters: Comparing the traits of Growing and Declining Mainline Protestant Church Attendees and Clergy," in the *Review of Religious Research*, Volume 58, Issue 4 (December 2016).

Weak Leaders make Weak Churches?

Dr. Sam Reimer, Crandall University, Moncton, New Brunswick

"I don't know why anyone would come to our church." The pastor's voice faltered as he tried to control his emotions. "The music is terrible, sometimes there is no one there who even plays an instrument. People visit and they don't come back." It was 1995 in Minneapolis, Minnesota. I was interviewing pastors as part of my Ph.D. research. I had called this pastor several times, but he refused to meet with me in person. I think he was too ashamed. He could not understand how anyone could be interested in doing research in his church. He had 30 older people attending, and he knew his church was dying. He was convinced it was his fault. A few days later, I spoke to another pastor of a much larger church in the same denomination who supported that view. "He has no clue what to do with that church," he stated emphatically.

I felt the grief of this pastor of the dying church. He was at his wit's end. He knew he needed younger families, better music, and maybe even better preaching to attract new people, but he couldn't make it happen. Was it his fault?

Over the past two decades, I have interviewed hundreds of Protestant pastors/priests and denominational leaders in both Canada and the U.S. Many of these leaders seem convinced that the key to flourishing churches is leadership: Strong leadership. Leadership that promotes a compelling vision that the laity can own and rally around; leadership that mobilizes the congregants to serve in their gifting; leadership that is innovative and understands how to lead change; and leadership that motivates church members to reach out into their communities.

Such pastoral leadership is not easy to come by. In fact, a shortage of good leadership is a major concern for all the evangelical denominational leaders we interviewed. Their pastors were aging, there were fewer young people going to seminary, and fewer seminary grads were becoming church pastors. Added to this, some young pastors would leave the ministry. Our research showed that younger pastors were less satisfied with their churches than their older counterparts, maybe because they had less desirable churches, and maybe because church leadership was not what they hoped it would be.

While denominational leaders focus on internal factors (inside the church walls), sociologists are more likely to focus on external factors, like the community or the country in which the church is located. They would argue that external factors are more powerful predictors of church growth than internal factors. Sociologists, using their fancy statistical models, find that the growth or decline of the community around the church is more important than leadership. One should also look to see if there are a lot of similar churches around that will compete for members. The religious vibrancy of the national or regional culture matters too. In Canada, where people have decreasing interest in institutional religion, it's hard to attract people to church, regardless of how beautiful the building, how great the programs, how wonderful the music and preaching, how welcoming the people, and how good the leadership.

Its been 20 years since I spoke to that defeated pastor in Minneapolis, and I still remember him. I wonder if any leader could have re-energized that church.

Does leadership matter? Of course, it matters a lot. But external factors probably matter even more. I would hypothesize that good leadership is a necessary but not sufficient condition for flourishing churches. Churches need a sizable population nearby that can be attracted to their church, and less competition from similar churches and growing communities increase that pool of potential congregants. But without good leadership, that potential normally remains untapped. A gifted leader will rarely grow a flourishing congregation in a shrinking town that is already serviced by other churches. (Many other cultural and demographic factors matter as well). But poor leadership can keep a church in a growing suburban neighborhood from flourishing, even if there are no competing churches in the area. Flourishing congregations require both. We need to pay as much attention to the demographic and cultural context around a church, as we pay to what happens inside it.

Dr. Sam Reimer is author (along with Michael Wilkinson) of *Evangelical Congregations in Canada* (2015, McGill-Queen's).

Are We Embarrassed? The Under Use of Marketing in Congregations

Carla Leon, Manager of New Initiatives (EDGE – A Network for New Ministry & Ministry Renewal, The United Church of Canada)

Congregations undoubtedly do amazing work. We have health services, food banks, children's programming, leadership development, summer camps, long term care facilities, and programming to support every subsector of society with almost any challenge (not to mention supporting our communities with spiritual grounding, emotional support, and connection).

If we were for-profits with these fantastic results, we would be shouting this from the rooftop. Our people would brag about the cool company that they work for. Our advertising would show how much impact we have made. Our marketing messages would feature these amazing stories. We would have marketing!!

But this doesn't happen that often. Why not? The marketing challenge in congregations is 3-fold:

Humbleness. The value of being humble is ingrained in us. Shouldn't we do good things and be good people just for the sake of being good? Wouldn't it be bad if we wanted recognition for this work? This value holds us back from marketing.

We are introverts. It's true! A majority of congregational members are introverts. We love having one-on-one conversations that are genuine and safe. We are often social, but not overtly so. This natural inhibition to draw attention to ourselves holds us back from marketing.

Fear of rejection. We think that people don't want to hear our story and conversations about faith communities are taboo. So we don't bring it up! Interestingly enough, there is only a very small percentage of people who are actively unwilling to hear stories from a faith community. Most people are interested and willing to listen. It is this small group of negative people that holds many congregations back from marketing.

There are many reasons out there for congregations to avoid marketing. However, there is a very real ethical dilemma in not telling our story and not marketing. If we aren't telling everyone that we know about the amazing work that we are doing, then people can't benefit from it. **People aren't being cared for, because we aren't marketing!!**

With this logic, we have to start marketing. We need to start telling our family & friends, using traditional community channels, and learning about best practices. When marketing is used by flourishing congregations, there can be fantastic results: a) **Public relations & press interest starts happening.** This is the best marketing, because it is free! Once you are on the news agencies' list, they will contact you for news ideas and will quote you on other topics which gets your name out even more; b) **Partnership opportunities appear!** Once you are on the community's radar, more opportunities follow.

Start communicating about your great work now & get on people's radars. Small wins lead to bigger wins. Once the momentum starts, it gets a lot easier.

Can You Imagine A Church Where....

Jamie Holtom, Minister North Bramalea United Church in Brampton

I don't know about you but sometimes I forget why I got into this in the first place. Sometimes I find I can lose my way and get focused on the wrong things. Sometimes it just seems like we are busy being busy and have forgotten the business we're actually in!

Ever felt that way?!

Fortunately there are other times too though ...

Times where I can imagine and see a different reality, a church that is growing people into mature followers of Jesus and truly experiencing the power of God's transforming powers.

Can you imagine that?

Can you imagine a church that is alive with people who pray every day?

Can you imagine all kinds of people, coming to church on a Sunday morning so excited to worship God that you can just feel the energy rise as they enter?

Can you imagine a church where people love each other and share their life together in real and authentic ways?

Can you imagine a church where people love to serve and are growing in their relationship with Jesus as they use the gifts God has given them?

Can you imagine a church filled with people who love to give generously so much so that the offering plates overflow each week?

Can you imagine a church where people are so in awe of God and what God is doing in their own lives that they can't help but share their faith and invite their friends?

Can you imagine a church like this?

As we imagined a church like this we started to think about a way to help people grow in the way of Jesus. As we began to imagine a church like this we knew we needed to get even more intentional about discipleship and clarifying what it looked like to follow Jesus.

After a lot of prayer and conversation our worship team came up with the following "targets:"

- Spiritual practices (spending time with God each day);
- Worshipping together weekly;
- Authentic community;
- Serving;
- Giving generously; wnr
- Sharing Christ.

We called it "Bullseye: Aiming to Follow Jesus"

These targets have offered our church something to aim for, a life where we are certainly a work in progress, but at least have some clarity on what this Christian life might look like.

And we have discovered that as people commit to living this way and practicing these six markers somehow God is up to something good.

It's good to have a target!

Which one of the six targets above has helped you grow in your relationship with God? Which has been the most challenging? What about for your church?

Canada's Catholics: A Flourishing Church in Need of Flourishing Parishes

Reginald W. Bibby, Professor of Sociology, University of Lethbridge

Catholics are readily Canada's largest religious group, numbering some 13 million people. That works out to about 40% of the Canadian population, compared to around 25% for Protestants and 10% for Other Major Faiths, led by Muslims at 3%. The balance of the population – almost 25% – indicate that they have no religion.

Yet, as the 21st century began, Catholic parishes in Canada were not particularly flourishing. According to those most actively involved, 25% of their congregations had been growing in recent years. But some 40% reported that their groups had been declining, while the remaining 35% indicated that things had remained about the same. Outside Quebec, the three category breakdowns were about one-third, one-third, and one-third. In Quebec, only 10% of active respondents reported that their congregations had been growing, although another 30% said the as of 2015, had been getting smaller.

There are signs that things are looking up, especially outside Quebec. According to Catholic Parish Numerical Trends: 2000 and 2015 (%) as reported by regular attendees, the new numerical norm for Catholic parishes is stability and growth (75%) rather than decline. And in Quebec, the decline level of 60% has fallen to about 35%, with stability now at 55%. Growth is still largely elusive, but nonetheless is being realized in about 1 in 10 parish instances.

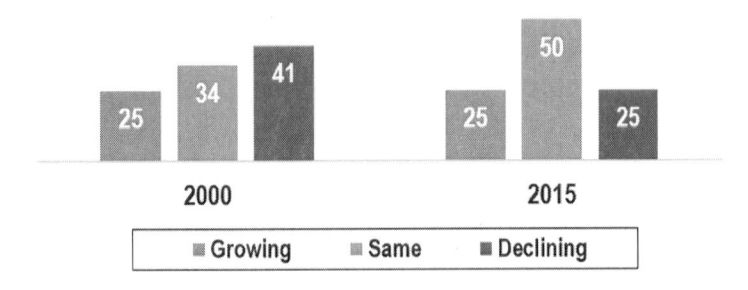

Catholic Parish Numerical Trends: 2000 and 2015 (%)
As Reported by Regular Attendees

	2000	2015
Growing	25	25
Same	34	50
Declining	41	25

A major reason for the recent rise in Catholic parish growth and stability is immigration. As most readers know, there has been a global explosion in the growth of religion, led by Christianity and Islam. According to the reputable Pew Research Forum, Christians and Muslims will each number some 3 billion people by 2050 – roughly twice their 1950 totals. That world-wide expansion is already having a profound impact on religion in Canada as newcomers arrive from elsewhere. Of major importance, Statistics Canada tells us that, in the next several decades, immigration figures will reach unprecedented levels as Canada attempts to sustain its population size in the face of an insufficient level of natural increase.

In the process, immigration is almost single-handedly transforming the religious situation in Canada. So much for the idea that religion's days were numbered. In the last decade alone, new arrivals included a whopping 500,000 Catholics, along with some 400,000 Muslims and about 200,000 people with varied

"Christian" ties. Further illustrating the diverse religious appetites of immigrants, about 450,000 of those who came arrived with "No Religion."

The large infusion of Catholics from other countries is having a significant impact on parishes. Of considerable importance, the new arrivals – led by Filipinos – are typically more devout and more involved than their Canadian-born counterparts. While 25% of Catholics born in Canada are attending services at least once a month, the figure for those born outside Canada is a stunning 55%.

As a result, Catholic parish numbers and religious commitment are both on the rise. And parishes and Dioceses are becoming more culturally diverse, with that diversity often extending to theological and social attitudes and practices as well.

In short, adjustment issues notwithstanding – including the heightened need for human and financial resources – Catholic parishes and Dioceses in Canada are becoming more robust and healthy. In places like Vancouver, Surrey, Edmonton, Calgary, Winnipeg, Toronto, Markham, and Montreal, large Asian and multicultural parishes are thriving. In Toronto alone, mass is celebrated in some 40 languages every Sunday in 240 parishes, and one new mega-church with seating for more than 1,000 people has been established every year for the last fifteen years.

Still, large numbers of Catholics have minimal involvement with parishes. Since the 1960s, nation Catholic weekly attendance has dropped from around 80% to 20% – and to less than 10% in Quebec. Nevertheless, some 80% of Catholics everywhere in Canada maintain that they attend mass at least occasionally. At

Christmas, for example, attendance levels rise to about 50%, reaching around 35% in Quebec and 65% elsewhere.

Yet, the fact that more people – especially Canadian-born Catholics – are not actively involved suggests that many parishes could use considerable help in becoming flourishing congregations. As of 2015, Angus Reid and I found that 30% of Catholics who currently are attending services less than once a month indicate that they would be open to more involvement if they "found it worthwhile." The levels are 47% outside Quebec, and a much-lower, 15% in Quebec. People tell us they are typically looking to have various spiritual, personal, and relational needs addressed.

Clearly all of us give our time and resources to those things that enhance our lives and the lives of those we care about most. It's noteworthy that Catholics who are involved in their parishes speak of the spiritual and personal enrichment that such participation brings. If less-involved Catholics can likewise find that greater ties with parishes tangibly contributes to their lives, additional numbers can be expected to want to have more to do with parishes and the Church more generally. Currently, however, most are not experiencing that connection, especially in Quebec.

Hopefully one of the priorities of *The Flourishing Churches Institute* will be to actively engage Catholics. They need all the help they can get in creating flourishing parishes that can be responsive to the thousands of people who will be arriving in Canada over the next few decades – as well as ministering well to the millions of Catholics who need to find significance in parish life.

The need and the opportunity are obvious.

Lost in a crowd?

Dr. David Eagle, Research Associate with the Clergy Health Initiative at Duke Divinity School

Lakewood Church in Houston, TX. [Photo by Amber Case. This work is licensed under a Creative Commons Attribution-NonCommercial 2.0 Generic License available here]

While they've been around for a long time, mega-churches have grown in popularity and influence. The Leadership Network reports that in Canada there are about 150 churches with weekly worship attendance of 1,000 or more. Together, these congregations draw 300,000 Canadians to worship each week. When we think about flourishing churches, it's worth asking: are large churches necessarily flourishing churches?

In some ways, yes. Data collected by the Leadership Network suggest that at a time when most churches in Canada are struggle to maintain their current size, large churches are growing. Not only that, but large churches are more ethnically diverse than small churches – certainly an indicator of health in a diverse country like Canada. And, large churches offer a wide array of programs and services both to their members and their communities – another indicator of a flourishing congregation.

But in other ways, large churches can fail to flourish. They can struggle shaping and forming disciples. Over a hundred years ago, the German sociologist Georg Simmel made an important point about large versus small organizations. The larger an organization gets, the harder it is to influence people's behavior and beliefs. In my own research, I confirmed this trend exists in churches: The larger a church gets, the much less likely someone will attend weekly. To put some numbers behind this trend, if you take a person who is a weekly attender at a church with 100 attenders, there's only a 62% chance this person will be a weekly attender in a church of 10,000. While attendance is only one measure of discipleship, it is a key component. Becoming a disciple requires regular fellowship.

So, why do people attend large churches less frequently? Well, I think it boils down to one basic dynamic: in a big church, your comings and goings aren't noticed as much as in a smaller church. In a church of several thousand, you probably won't face the same encouragement (or the same pressures) to attend as in a church of 100. For large congregations, this has some important implications.

To begin with, one implication is that the kinds of people who are attracted to larger congregations might be more reluctant to become full and active participants. People who want a more anonymous environment or feel they don't have enough time to attend weekly services may in fact gravitate to bigger churches. This means that large churches need to be aware that the kinds of people they attract might need extra encouragement to get involved in the life of the congregation.

Another implication is that large churches are harder places to get involved in. People looking for a place to be involved are less likely to find the connections they need to plug in. So, what can larger churches do to confront these challenges? Here are a few suggestions:

1. Recognize that being large or small isn't bad or good, it just presents a different set of challenges and opportunities.
2. Find ways to make the church smaller. Think about creative ways to get newcomers into these smaller spaces.
3. Train a core group of your people to be fearless agents of hospitality. In a large church, it can be hard to spot newcomers. It's embarrassing to welcome someone who turns out to be a longtime attender.

Flourishing churches can be big, small and everything in between! But, across the board, flourishing churches are aware of the special opportunities and challenges that their size presents. While common ingredients exist, the recipe for promoting belonging looks different in a megachurch than it does in a small country congregation.

What is Truth? (Hint: It's more than Statistics)

Dr. Kevin Flatt, Associate Professor of History, Redeemer University

In 1963 the Anglican Church of Canada commissioned the prominent, pithy journalist Pierre Berton to tell them, from an outsider's perspective, exactly what was wrong with Canada's churches and what they needed to do to fix it.

In the resulting book, *The Comfortable Pew* (1965), Berton took the churches to task for being too attached to old dogmas like Jesus' resurrection, the Apostles' Creed, and even the idea of God as a cosmic "daddy on a cloud." In a modern age of rapid change, Berton wrote, Christians needed to abandon such primitive thinking. In the late twentieth century it would be "almost impossible" for faith to survive if it was based on traditional beliefs.

The book was a runaway bestseller and was highly praised by mainline church leaders, especially from the United and Anglican churches. His advice suited their convictions very well, and by and large their churches have been following it quite closely for the past half century.

It seems like reasonable advice, right? Don't we all need to keep up with the times?

The thing is, it didn't work. Quite the opposite, in fact: the more closely churches followed Berton's advice, the more they hemorrhaged people. The Anglicans peaked in 1964, the United Church in 1965. Since then they have lost well over half their membership.

Meanwhile, churches that defied Berton—relatively small conservative Protestant groups like the Fellowship Baptists, the Mennonite Brethren, and the Pentecostals—doubled or tripled in size in the same period. These churches held very tightly indeed to their traditional theological beliefs, especially the ones Berton thought were most embarrassing.

Historical evidence from the United States over the past two centuries shows a similar general pattern. Growth has favoured the more theologically conservative Protestant groups—that is, groups that see the Bible as trustworthy and accurate and base their theology on this.

But is this still true today? And does it apply at the level of individual churches? Here things get murkier. Some research has said yes, other research no.

Although the vast majority of mainline Protestant congregations in Canada are shrinking, a handful are growing. What makes them different? My colleagues Dave M. Haskell and Stephanie Burgoyne and I set out to answer this question.

Among other things, we found that the theological conservatism of both clergy and people were strongly positively linked with growth, even when a wide range of other factors were held constant. Other factors, like emphasis on youth ministry and accessible worship styles, were also important. Some of our results have recently been published in the *Review of Religious Research*, and Prof. Haskell has written about them on this blog.

Ever since we began presenting these findings, we have experienced a powerful backlash from some people. A lot of this backlash targets, not our methods or data, but things people *think* we are saying. We hear things like:

- "You can't judge the truth of a theology based on numbers." (We agree).
- "You can't expect churches to change their beliefs in order to grow." (Ditto).

When we're speaking as social scientists, our job is to understand and describe what's going on, not to tell people what they *should* be doing. Evidence linking conservative theology to growth doesn't prove that conservative theology is true, or that churches should adopt it.

Frankly, it's unrealistic to think that someone could completely reverse their beliefs because it might make their church grow. A dyed-in-the-wool theological liberal is not going to say, "I need to believe that Jesus physically rose from the dead if I want more church members? Gee, I guess I'll do that."

We take the old-fashioned view that people should believe the things they think are *true*, not the things they think will get bums in pews. While each of us on this research team have our own theological convictions (including profound disagreements), we don't think this kind of research can or should convince people to change theirs.

So if we aren't saying that, what *are* we saying?

First, we're saying that churches' beliefs do matter. They have effects. And different kinds of beliefs produce different effects, even if it's unpopular to point that out.

Second, we're adding our findings to a heap of evidence that Berton and others like him (e.g., John Spong) were simply empirically wrong in their predictions. Neither history nor sociology supports the claim that churches need to abandon traditional beliefs to survive and flourish.

Trying to figure out what to believe? Don't be swayed too much by Berton and other prophets of relevance. Don't let social scientists or church growth gurus drive the bus, either. Statistics have their uses, but identifying theological truth is not one of them.

Section III

flourishing
CONGREGATIONS INSTITUTE

Flourishing Congregations in Canada: Preliminary Observations

A Paper Presented by Joel Thiessen, Arch Wong, Bill McAlpine, and Keith Walker at the Flourishing Congregations Institute Launch, Ambrose University, Calgary, Alberta on November 26, 2016

Flourishing Congregations in Canada: Preliminary Observations

AMBROSE UNIVERSITY

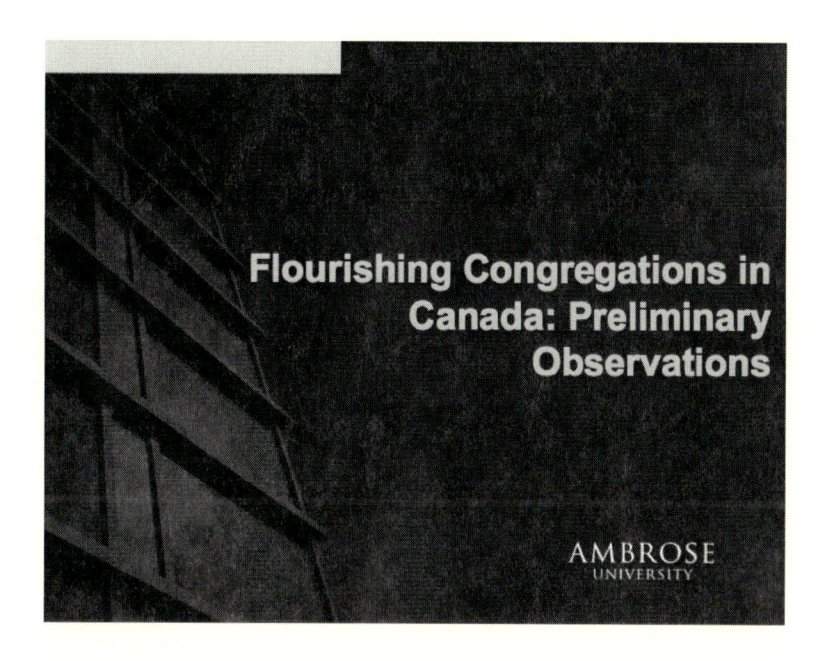

Introduction

Our aim in this session is to take a 39,000 foot altitude approach to explore how leaders in Catholic, mainline, and conservative Protestant congregations conceptualize what a flourishing congregation looks like (or ought to look like) in a Canadian context. In pursuing this task we make two assumptions.

First, we are presenting leader perceptions of flourishing congregations. At this point in the study our research team cannot state with confidence what traits are actually and commonly evident in congregations that are flourishing. So far our research as been delimited to the window afforded by about 100 academics, denominational and congregation leaders. We can only state: "this is what a select set of leaders have reported to us about their congregations and experiences." We will have more to say about this as we engage in other research methods (e.g., ethnographic, survey) and with a range of other participants (e.g., congregants, first hand observers). For example, if one of the leaders we interviewed identified diversity as a desirous trait of a flourishing congregation and claimed that their congregation is diverse, a sociologist might ask: How do congregants perceive and experience this or other kinds of diversity? Do members of different subgroups sit beside one another on Sunday mornings, or interact with one another in various ministry settings? What attitudes and behaviours does one find among congregants regarding other subgroups in the congregation? Later we talk about phase two and three in this project, which will help us to test the suggested perceptions and insights gleaned from phase one. Once more, this is merely a preliminary preview of some of our initial findings.

Introduction

- How do leaders in Catholic, mainline and conservative Protestant congregations conceptualize what a "flourishing congregation" looks like (or ought to look like) in a Canadian context?
    - *Presenting leader perceptions*
    - *Discussing "ideal types" – does not actually exist in reality*

AMBROSE
UNIVERSITY

Second, the traits and characteristics associated with flourishing congregations that we will discuss depict what Max Weber (1949), one of the founders of sociology, called "ideal types." An ideal type is a literary construct or expression of a particular concept; it may not actually exist in reality, but serves as an analytical description, explanation, measure, and representation of a concept resembling what might be found in concrete cases. Ideal types are useful points of when one begins to explore concepts to possibly refine, clarify, and develop more precise understandings and measurements. Importantly, these ideal types are not intended to be normative or evaluative. In other words, we do not claim that a leader's definition or description of "a" of flourishing congregation is better or worse than definition or description of "b." We have simply developed "ideal types" or features of flourishing congregations based on what we heard leaders telling us. Of course, it is highly unlikely that there are any congregations that embody each and all traits associated with any ideal type (as interviewees clearly stated to us).

Early and Selective Findings

The following sections capture how interviewees conceptualized and operationalized what a "flourishing congregation" looked like to them. Given the preliminary nature of our analysis we hold these categorizations and descriptions rather loosely. Admittedly it is difficult to conclude whether or not these characteristics are precursors or conditions for a congregation to flourish. Perhaps some are the results manifest in congregations that flourish or perhaps the types and indicators should be seen as representing some combination of traits and states. Moreover, without probing further in phase two and three of this study (see "Looking Forward" section), it is hard to assess whether these are lived realities, aspirational goals, beliefs and values or a blend of the three. If they are lived realities or aspirational goals these can be empirically measured. If they are intrinsic values that are held dear by our participants, these become a bit more difficult to measure. Last, we are cognizant that the ways that congregation-based and denominational leaders describe flourishing congregations may reveal specific theological, sociological, and practical assumptions and commitments. Part of our task in this project will be to clearly identify the varied and interrelated ways that these emerge.

Not Numbers … Or is it?

In many of our focus groups and interviews, one of the initial responses to the question "what comes to mind when you hear the phrase flourishing congregation" pertained to the size of a congregation. Some were quick to separate or decouple the notion of flourishing from the relative size of a congregation. A United Church of Canada minister in Halifax stated:

> I think we have to decouple flourishing from numbers. I'm not averse to numbers but I'm concerned that in our society what gets counted is the only thing that seems to matter. And there may be places that are flourishing where it's not possible for there to be numerical growth. The reality for the Maritimes is rural depopulation and that's true in other places as well. And it's possible for there to be flourishing congregations where there simply isn't the base for there to be a rapid growth in numbers. I think that the body continues to replicate and add to itself, but if we're only counting numbers we may be missing something.

Here we see an example of how, particularly for congregations in rural contexts and in the Maritimes, environmental conditions, such as declining population, contribute to a congregation's realities and how this, in turn, shapes how they think about what constitutes flourishing.

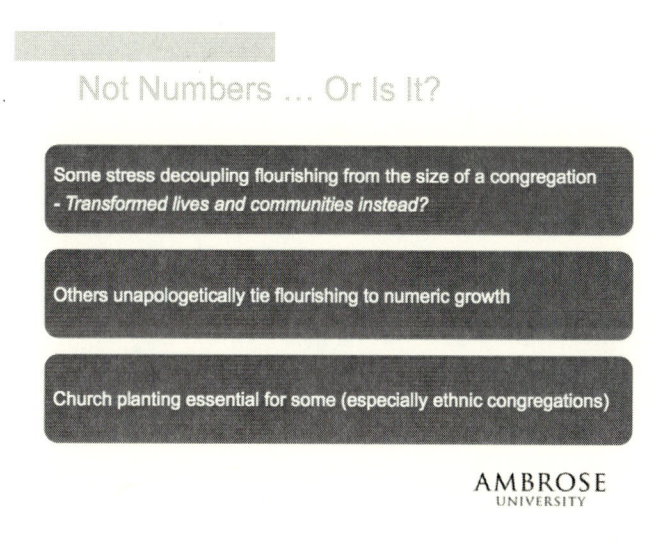

Not Numbers ... Or Is It?

- Some stress decoupling flourishing from the size of a congregation - *Transformed lives and communities instead?*
- Others unapologetically tie flourishing to numeric growth
- Church planting essential for some (especially ethnic congregations)

AMBROSE
UNIVERSITY

Others suggested that rather than measuring flourishing by numbers, one ought to look at transformed lives and communities. One church leader, reflective of others, signaled, "I would say it's not numeric. It's about people attending to what matters most, people being engaged, people being hoping, people owning their own faith, people celebrating that, people working to make the world a better place." A denominational leader in the Presbyterian Church of Canada revealed:

> I'm not convinced that [numbers are] as key anymore ... It's more fundamental than that. And so the transformational model of churches, incarnational churches they sometimes call them, I think becomes the more key approach I think for a vital church for now and for the future. When people in the

wider community see Christians changing because they believe that God has influenced their lives or if they see these Christians going out and giving up their time and their money and effort to make a change in the community, then both those roots are providing kind of an evidence for the existence of God.

Conversely, other leaders are adamant that a congregation that is not growing numerically – measured by things such as church attendance, membership or adherence, baptisms, conversions, or financial donations – is not flourishing. A leader of a conservative Protestant congregation with over 600 weekly attenders reflected, "In many ways I would say we believe that qualitative growth ultimately must show itself in quantitative growth." A Catholic priest in Alberta said:

> I think the first thing you would think of in a flourishing congregation would be the number, the attendees, the flourishing, we always think quantity … as much as we would like to detach those material things from what we would consider a flourishing church, community or congregation, when a group is flourishing, there will be manifestations and often it is in numbers, often it is in the sense of service, what they offer to the community. So you can't help but connect those things that when a group is flourishing, you would need a bigger space, you would have more services to offer, the following would be larger and growing, there would be more programs that are truly helpful in empowering these people into Christian faith. So yeah, that would go hand in hand.

Of course, this narrative that associates flourishing with numbers is easier for some. Most Catholic leaders that we interviewed highlighted the following sentiment: "Oftentimes Catholics think in terms of let's set up a parish and people will come to us because it happens. We have no problems with our numbers." A Catholic priest in British Columbia said, "We're not too worried about growth really. I mean it's going to grow, but we're not focused a lot." We heard countless narratives of Catholic parishes with well over 1000+ weekly attenders where their greatest concern was not having enough seats for all those who want to attend mass. In reality, Catholics have the stronghold of mega-churches in Canada (2000+ weekly attenders), or at the very least large churches (1000+), which warrants extensive research moving forward (see Bibby & Reid 2016). The reasons? Catholic schools are believed to link students and their families to regular mass attendance, and immigration; themes that we will explore in greater detail later.

The phenomenon of flourishing churches planting churches is a noticeable refrain among some representing congregations who value quantitative metrics. This was most common among newer church plants and with some ethnic congregations who we encountered in our first phase of research. For instance, some leaders shared that two churches were birthed out of their congregation in the past five years, and their goal was to birth another two in the next five years. A pastor of a multiethnic congregation in Ontario stated that his congregation "basically just exists to multiply – to just keep giving birth. Even as they plant, they already have a strategy to plant within a year or two again. And it's that whole concept. It's not a church that is worried about, 'okay how we pay the bills or how we pay this or that to survive.' It's a multiplying concept."

Several questions arise for us. We plan to delve into these as this study progresses: What are the underlying narratives at work between the two differing expressions of flourishing here? Are smaller congregations less inclined to associate numeric growth with flourishing with vice versa among larger congregations, or is there a more nuanced middle position? Are some seeking to detach Canadian understandings of flourishing from perceived American ones; where mega-churches are far more common? Do denominational and church leaders distance themselves from numbers as a way to psychologically cope with the reality that their congregations, and many around them, struggle to sustain numbers or grow numerically? Or are there possible theological reasons for connecting or disconnecting flourishing from numeric growth?

Clear Self Identity

Clear Self Identity

- Clear articulation of who they are and are not
  - *Rooted, in part, in the spiritual life*
- Is it possible to have a clear self identity and not flourish?

AMBROSE
UNIVERSITY

A unifying narrative among many of the leaders who we interacted with involved the possession of a clear self-identity. These congregations were described as having a firm grasp of who they were and what the congregation was, is, and aspires to be. For the leaders that we heard that, a clear self-identity included a realization that congregations do not strive to become like the church down the road nor do they try to be all things to all people; they are unique in some respects. To this end several shared that their identity might be captured on a t-shirt or a bus advertisement, ensuring that their core purpose was memorable. By extension participants indicated that congregations who are not clear on their central purpose and identity struggle to flourish, especially in a Canadian context where many congregations fight to remain relevant and keep the doors open in a progressively secular setting. This Catholic leader spoke about congregational identity in this way:

> When you develop a sense of identity, you begin to have that sense of conviction, sense of direction. It helps you in your leadership. You can't help but grow. People find it attractive when a group or a person knows what it's all about right? And they want to belong to something that they can relate to. And they do tend to be hospitable because people who know themselves as an organization, I think will truly want to reach out and share the good news. A vibrant spiritual life must and should be a given in a Christian context because that is what we're about. I think that self-formation and self-identity is really key. Congregations who say yes to everything and who can't say no because they are so afraid of hurting emotions, are usually the ones who suffer because they have no self-identity. They just want to be everything to everyone. And it's also dangerous to spiritual life because if you're to follow Christ, Christ did not say yes to everything as well. Christ had a very strong handle on what's good, bad, what's right, wrong, and he

led people. So, that is critical, that self-identity, because if you know who you are and you're secure about it, then everything else just flows. But if you're constantly searching and you can't make a decision, none of these would ever happen.

As for the content of a congregation's identity and raison d'être, this varied. We heard responses that ranged from theological particulars, to an ethnic or multiethnic focus, to a neighbourhood or parish church, to a single or multigenerational congregation, to an evangelistic emphasis, among other areas. Yet one recurring theme arose across the theological continuum: a congregation's identity is rooted in the spiritual life, in various religious beliefs and practices, and ultimately around Jesus. For instance, Catholics in this research singled out the sacraments of the Church as core to congregational identity. A conservative Protestant leader in Ontario proclaimed, "I think there is an identity being rooted in Jesus. They have that very clear sense of their identity as a congregation extending from Jesus, mission, life, presence among them." We say more about these identity markers in the next section on "vibrant spiritual life."

Still, not all participants agreed with a blanket correlation between clear self-identity and congregations that flourish. One focus group participant carefully noted that congregations may have a clear self-identity yet not flourish: "If you look at [the traits] without the descriptors, [they] could actually be a symptom of an unflourishing church … so I've met congregations on the verge of closure that have a clear self-identity." The inference was that a congregation's self-identity could be anchored around beliefs and practices that do not generate numeric growth or healthy organizational dynamics or transformed individuals. This begs the question: are there certain beliefs, practices, structures, and/or ideologies that bind flourishing congregations together? Can one advance the case that while congregations often have what they deem to be a unique self-identities, there are shared identity-related realities that bind many churches together? Thus far, our sense is that at the macro-level there are some unifying commonalities in how church leaders think about the identity of flourishing congregations. The remaining observations capture these similarities across traditions and regions. We eventually hope to articulate differences across traditions and regions too, though it is too early to say anything substantive about this yet.

Vibrant Collective Spiritual Life

A cornerstone feature of a congregation's identity is its value for and opportunities to develop a vibrant collective spiritual life; in the words of one leader, "to smell like Jesus" (this statement is full of meaning and assumptions that we intend to probe further as this research project develops). We listened to a range of stories detailing the role that prayer, Scripture, the Eucharist, the Holy

Spirit, fasting, and other spiritual disciplines reportedly play for leaders and their congregants in flourishing congregations. Reinforcing earlier literature on congregations that are theologically oriented in a conservative direction, a recent study of mainline Protestant congregations in Canada reveals that those churches that are growing score notably higher on various religious/spiritual belief and practice indicators compared with congregations that are declining (Haskell, Flatt & Burgoyne 2016). For instance, some interviewees identified seasons of intense prayer and fasting as catalysts for flourishing in their contexts. Two specific themes stand out to us regarding a vibrant collective spiritual life: religious experience and transformed lives.

Participants expressed that flourishing congregations created opportunities for individuals to meaningfully experience God; these were centrally available to congregants in weekly services. Several interviewees spoke about a distinct energy that was felt in flourishing congregations in weekly services, though few described what this "energy" looked or felt like – one would just know it when they sensed it. A United Church of Canada minister expressed that, "It just has energy. You feel it." For Catholic leaders, a purposeful, thoughtful, and considered liturgy (with the highpoint of the Eucharist) stood out above all things for the vibrant collective spiritual life. One Catholic priest, characteristic of several of his peers, shared the following question and response concerning people experiencing God in weekly Mass:

> How can we create an atmosphere where we can provide a God-moment encounter for people walking through the front door? So whether it's as soon as they grab that front door and they walk in, there's got to be a feeling there in the air from the person they first meet to get a smile, to perhaps it's the

way that the worship happens or if it's a special event and it's the music and it's the message. So it all comes back to where can we reach them where they're at; so that they are touched by the Spirit; and then, how do we recognize what the next thing is that they need so that they can start to conform, be drawn to the Lord? So I just throw that out there for ourselves is when someone has a God moment, lives change ... I think that that's still an important thing to try and facilitate the God moment.

The end of this statement captures the sentiments of many who we interviewed, that meaningful experiences with God leads to transformed lives. Expressed differently, while denominational and congregational leaders are interested in helping congregants foster attitudes and behaviours associated with a vibrant collective spiritual life, the ultimate expression of a vibrant spiritual life is a transformed personal life. An Anglican leader described the following goal in their congregation's activities:

Lives changed; changed lives, for me. It's not about being friendly. I can go to the rotary club, find friendly people. I need to see, the litmus test for me is, is your life changed? Is it growing? Are you grounded? Is there maturity? Is there sanctification? ... I mean people just said, 'I wasn't coming to church and I've been here for a year and a half. My life is so different it's just amazing.' Whether we get those stories out, that is an encouragement to me; that maybe people are able to deliver about those testimonies and how they're done. But the point is it's happening. For me that's one of the things I'm looking for ... I need to see lives change because I see so much broken, otherwise. That's it.

One of our central aims for later phases of this research will entail a broader and deeper examination of various religious beliefs and practices among congregants themselves.

Discipleship

Discipleship

- Disciples making disciples
- Clearly articulated pathway and process for discipleship
- Concern about how to define and implement discipleship (and processes) remain

AMBROSE
UNIVERSITY

One of the earliest observations offered by several participants in our research was that flourishing congregations "produce disciples." Several congregations that we encountered expressed a desire for their church to embody something akin to the following approach by a conservative Protestant congregation in Calgary:

> The way we program our teaching, the way we outline our schedule and the way we teach our leaders and coach our leaders towards how they lead their organization, how they lead their part of the organization, their small group or their serve team or whatever we call them, that would be it. And I think that fundamentally shifted four years ago when we really

decided, you know, discipleship. We want to see every person in our church making a disciple. That's our vision statement. Not anything other than that. So that means every person has a job. Everyone has a role. And it's very clearly what we're building; we're building disciples. And not discipleship as defined as people who have made a commitment to Jesus, but discipleship defined as an entire spectrum from the anti-theist to the apostolic leader.

Some denominational and congregational leaders articulated a specific pathway to "disciple" members of their congregation. These processes involved members moving their way through various courses, volunteer initiatives, and shared church-wide experiences into deeper commitments in their faith tradition and with their fellow congregants. It is important to note here that discipleship was understood by many as a lifelong process; where one is constantly "being discipled" and growing in their faith, whether as a recent convert or someone who had been a Christian for five decades.

At the same time many expressed that discipleship was the crux of their challenge. This was heightened in a modern and secular Canada with many competing narratives for people's allegiances and where there may be diminished levels of commitment to congregational life. They grappled with how best to define and measure discipleship in 21st Century Canada. Most troubling to many, how does a congregation actually disciple people in the faith? A Catholic priest in Ontario outlined his desires for his congregation to grow in its discipleship capacity:

What I would like it to look like is, that the parishioners have a real sense of their discipleship. That they are disciples. And that in the living out of their lives, whether it's in the context of their family, their work, or their school, they see the way that they live, the way that they engage in a relationship is an expression of their relationship with the person of Jesus. And that they're living that relationship so that they have a sense of their own – that they are disciples with call to make Christ present in the world. If everybody in my parish had that understanding and appreciation of who they are of their identity, then I would say that would be a very positive parish.

Upon sharing these things, this leader suggested that his congregation was far too consumer-oriented toward their religious beliefs and practices and that they were unwilling to incur the costs and sacrifice necessary to be "true disciples." This latter reflection is significant because it reveals that even those who defined their congregations as flourishing still saw areas and opportunities for growth and development. Part of our objective, as this research develops, is to carefully examine the specific processes, pathways, and narratives that congregations use for discipleship. We also want to explore the relationship between discipleship and other aspects of flourishing congregational life delineated in this paper.

Leadership

Leadership
- Organizational culture for leadership success
- Lay leadership, collaborative leadership, and leadership development
  - "Yes" culture; Hiring from within
- Spirit-led leadership
- Strategic leadership – "let leaders lead"

Previous literature has been clear that leadership is an important variable to consider for congregations to flourish (e.g., Bickers 2005; Dudley & Johnson 1993; Holling 2001; Parson & Leas 1993; Roozen & Hadaway 1993; Saarinen 1986; Scheitle & Dougherty 2008; Stark & Finke 2000; Wilkes 2001a, 2001b). Four aspects to leadership stand out in our early analysis.

First, strategic leadership appears to be a strength possessed by many of those who we interviewed where church structures and polity and congregants enabled and "let leaders lead." A conservative Protestant pastor in Ontario compared flourishing congregations with those who were not thriving in the following way: "Strategic leadership … the majority of churches don't know how to do it … The churches that are succeeding, all of them, have strategic leaders who know how to line up the dots … How to get there. That's it. That's what strategy is. And across the country I'd say that majority of pastors are not strategic. They grab this and it didn't work, but they don't see that in itself it's just a tool. It's just a part of all the other tools and you've got to have a path that you choose to lead that strategy." Part of what we would like to eventually do, perhaps in a comparative context between flourishing and non-flourishing congregations, is test some of the assumptions made by this leader and others regarding strategic leadership.

Strategic leadership seemed to be manifest among leaders who had the posture and skillset to effectively lead an organization. Countless leaders who we spoke with claimed to have confidently and skillfully helped their congregation name and locate themselves from a branding and marketing perspective (identified by participants as a need in the Canadian religious marketplace where many Canadians have negative perceptions of religious organizations (see Angus Reid Institute 2015; Bibby 2011; Wilkins-Laflamme 2014). In turn these leaders described how strategic leadership was essential to guide their congregation through change and transition into new congregational realities and experiences. Interestingly, we discovered several books written by those that we interviewed, documenting their experiences, theology, and philosophy of church leadership.

Second, Catholic, mainline, and conservative Protestant denominational and church leaders frequently spoke about strong lay leadership, collaborative leadership, and/or cultivating a culture of leadership development in their organizations. Our team heard numerous narratives where congregants took an active role to shape the congregation's identity, vision, mission, dreaming, and activities. Many we interviewed were quick to point out their perception that Canadian congregations valued cooperation and consensus within and between congregations far more than those in the United States. In their eyes a congregation cannot realistically change or pursue its vision and mission without buy-in from those "on the ground." A leader from one of the Catholic Diocese visited offered the following reflections:

> One of things that is very striking about your average Roman Catholic congregation – the stereotype would suggest that the parish priest does everything. This story, my first months in this role, and I was calling around to the parish and really it was lay persons that was given power over these certain offices … the flourishing congregations are usually the ones that know how to designate, and designate well.

A conservative Protestant pastor shared this narrative with our research team:

> We just had a couple of – because we haven't had a property and facilities committee in place for a while – we had a single person trying to do this and it's a fairly substantial building to have one person do it. So we got this committee in place and put the right people around the table and shared their vision, launched it. And so I've been at the last two meetings and so they've got a meeting tonight and so I called them and said, 'I won't make it.' They said, 'Oh that's okay we don't want you there anyways.' And which is exactly what I've been hoping for.

Other leaders aspired for a denominational and congregational culture of shared leadership. An Anglican Bishop recalled the first few months in his new position:

> There's this high desire for the Bishop to make decisions for congregations. I don't wanna do that. Or I'm willing to play a kind of circuit breaker, intervener role as necessary. But as much as I can, I wanna hand our decisions to people … I think it is with as much power and authority given a Bishop. So the role of the Bishop is supposed to be a unifier. So when we commission new clergy, what is said in that service is that this is a ministry we share. The Bishop shares with the person, that priest. I mean it's wonderful to have that.

Strong lay involvement and leadership development partially explains why many of those interviewed claimed to cultivate a "yes" culture in their denominations and congregations (path-goal theory; see House 1996). House's path-goal theory stated that the leader motivates followers to accomplish identified objectives. He assumed that the effective leader has the skills to improve the motivation of followers by clarifying the paths and removing obstacles to high performance and desired objectives. As one example, a conservative Protestant leader in Calgary claimed, "We create a lot of freedom; we seek to create a lot of parameters. I want to say yes as much as I possibly can to requests and initiatives. We are not terribly afraid of failure, if something doesn't work, okay, we will learn, we will move on and try something new." We discovered time and again that denominational and congregational leaders said that they rarely put up roadblocks to ideas that emerged among those lower than them in the hierarchy. For example, denominations provided resources for new church plants to begin, and congregational leaders gave the laity freedom and permission to start new ministry areas. A "yes" narrative to trying new things looked to be essential to the DNA of many congregations that we were exposed to through their leaders. Conversely, several leaders demonized denominational and congregational structures that they believed stifled the prospect of organizational flourishing.

Amidst narratives on leadership development and a "yes" culture, there are some traditions that experience decline in membership, attendance, or financial giving. Interviewed leaders from this broader denominational reality of decline revealed an acute awareness that leadership development from within was an imperative for organizational vitality, sustainability, and longevity. A mainline Protestant denominational leader in the Maritimes highlighted this point in response to an ongoing crisis in her tradition:

> We have a number of parishes that are unable to afford full-time clergy leadership. And even some of the larger parishes that have had multiple staff are declining in number of staff. Instead of three clergy, they're at one or two or one and a half and that kind of thing. So we recognized the need to be more intentional about identifying lay leaders and empowering and releasing them. And we've really struggled with the priest does everything. And it is the center of the parish and if you don't have a priest, you're nothing. Don't have a full-time priest who lives in your community, you're nothing. So we're transitioning from that thankfully I think into a more Biblical model of really shared ministry and recognizing that.

This participant went on to describe the positive impact for congregations that had resulted from this intentional focus on leadership development.

In a slightly different vein, we also heard of multi-staff congregations, mostly conservative Protestant, hiring various staff from within their congregations. The belief was expressed that effective leadership is aided when hiring those who have a strong understanding of the local church's culture, and who have existing rapport and respect among congregants. In some cases congregations hired leaders from within with a succession plan in mind, where an associate pastor was hired with the long-range intent of this person eventually becoming the lead minister.

A third element of leadership that arose across traditions and regions was "spirit-led" leadership where leaders were seen as consciously being "in step" with where they believed God was leading their congregations. The following exchange in a focus group, initiated by a denominational leader, captured this point well:

> Churches that really flourish are churches were you sense the pastor has the ability to hear God's voice … there's an evidence that you are really being spirit led, not institutionally, denominational, leadership led. But that there's really a spiritual component to the leader that comes through really clearly. I mean that of all leadership, not just one who's preaching at the front. And I think people really rise up and respect that when they sense that- oh okay, hold on.

Another denominational leader affirmed this line of thinking in response:

> People need to know that you've been with God. You don't have to be alpha male, top dog, best strategic guy on the planet. They just want to know that you've been with God …

early on I thought it was competency that people wanted. And there is a threshold of competency that's needed. But after awhile it wasn't anything explicitly they said. You could tell they were looking for that.

A local pastor then interjected:

It's this responsiveness to the Spirit of God. And it's not just leaders. I look at our whole leadership team too. And this is something we're trying to cultivate, that discernment piece. Otherwise it's just Robert's Rules of Order ... procedure and process as opposed to, what is God up to? Are we discerning that piece and responsive to that?

In concrete terms those interviewed reported that an active prayer life was invaluable for religious leaders, along with being obedient to what they believe God was calling their congregation to be or do.

Fourth, many of those we interviewed were in organizational cultures that helped them to thrive personally and professionally. Leaders spoke of having some semblance of work-life balance, sabbaticals embedded into their work rhythm, personal and professional support and empowerment by their church governance, and training opportunities to hone their craft (e.g., formal education, courses, seminars, and books on leadership). Of note, participants who reflected on their own seminary training, highlighted the need for seminaries to offer required courses on leadership skills and development for clergy in school (among other skills, such as conflict resolution). Though not a focus in this paper, we encountered a number of clergy who had no formal religious education prior to assuming their current post as a lead or executive pastor. Instead these clergy had educational or professional experiences in business, marketing, or leadership. As one interviewee stated, "We're really seeing leaders that are being ordained are not necessarily equipped with all the skillsets that they need for today's context." At the denominational level some, like the following Anglican Diocese, were taking this development into their own hands: "We bring people together to learn about leadership and congregational development in teams from parishes."

Several questions arose regarding leadership that we intend to explore further as this research unfolds. For instance, what habits, experiences, or narratives may set strategic congregational leaders apart from leaders who are less strategic? Do congregants in flourishing congregations feel as empowered as the leaders in our current research suggested, and what are the processes and experiences of those who are being developed as leaders within local churches? What are the specific conditions, people, contexts, and structures under which leaders tend to say "yes" to other leaders in training or innovative ideas?

"Outside the Box"

"Outside the Box"

Entrepreneurial initiatives, risk-taking endeavours, and dreams

- Perhaps a response to secular context...

thinking THE BOX

AMBROSE
UNIVERSITY

Picking up on the "yes" ethos among leaders in flourishing congregations, several leaders from across the Christian spectrum and Canadian regions discussed the need and ability to think and act "outside the box" in order to flourish. One pastor articulated it this way: flourishing congregations have "the willingness to change. Letting things grow. There's no growth without change." We heard numerous stories of entrepreneurial initiatives, risk-taking endeavors, and dreams and schemes for the future, along with narratives that "failures" are seeds for new ideas and growth. One Anglican leader asserted, "I think a flourishing congregation is a congregation that can contemplate imaginatively a variety of different possibilities ... that imaginative capacity would be a starting place for me when I think of flourishing congregations." In one of our focus groups, one respondent declared, "Willingness to risk I think is probably something that's really important in flourishing congregations. It's okay to try something and have it not work." In response, another church leader at the table added, "Not working means that it didn't explode and there's not 500 people involved. Oh it was a failure, right? But it's getting over that and going sometimes things are only going to be a flash in the pan and they need to be for other things to happen. That's okay." To name a few examples, these "out of the box" initiatives included church planting ventures, new liturgical styles and expressions in worship services, purchasing multiple properties to provide social services in the community, or pouring funding into a ministry idea that may or may not be successful.

One possible way to account for the prevalence of risk-taking among flourishing congregations is the perceived dire state of the Christian Church in Canada in an increasingly secular context. Some persons in our research interactions suggested that Christianity was ever more marginalized in Canadian society than in the United States. As a result congregations simply could not continue to do things as they always had, in terms of expecting people to walk through the doors each week. Particularly observed in Vancouver, this compelled many, where over 40% of people say they have "no religion" (Statistics Canada 2013), to try all kinds of things because, in their words, "they had nothing to lose." As it turns out, we spoke to leaders of church plants birthed in the last two decades who now run weekly attendances in excess of 2,000 each week. They had incorporated all kinds of creative and innovative expressions for very specific niche markets (e.g., young professionals who live in high rise condominiums).

Hospitable Community

Hospitable Community

- People are loved and cared for, and seem to enjoy one another's company
- Clear processes for joining and remaining involved
- Pride in one's congregation

AMBROSE
UNIVERSITY

Sociologically, we know that social ties play an instrumental role in a person joining a religious community and remaining part of that group (see Stark & Bainbridge 1985; Stark & Finke 2000). As people feel accepted, loved, cared for, and embraced by people in a congregation, they are more likely to join and continue their association with that congregation. Most in our informants reported that their congregations were hospitable communities, where people genuinely enjoyed one another's company (an idea or claim that we will test with congregants in later phases of research). What stands out to us from our interviews are the processes that leaders identified as means to help people join and remain involved in their church. A conservative Protestant pastor stressed that their congregation has:

> A clear and effective model of ministry. Everyone's not just clear on who we are, where we're going conceptually, but how

this works. How our discipleship process works? How we reach people for Christ. How did people get integrated into our church? How do we launch people to live missionally? How does it work? What steps do you take? There's a very clear how between churches that are either not flourishing or aspiring to be flourishing. I encounter more churches that wish, that want to be flourishing but don't know how, than churches that are. And I don't think that the difference is motivational. The difference isn't that some churches want to be flourishing more than others. It's that some churches have figured out and engaged their people and how. And others haven't.

For instance, flourishing congregation leaders said that they had a clear and systematic process for identifying newcomers (we saw in-depth flow charts of such processes), making personal contact via telephone or coffee in the week following a first visit, and then helping newcomers to work their way into the congregational networks via small groups or volunteer opportunities. Unlike one or two generations ago, fewer Canadians have a Christian memory of any kind. Therefore, leaders of flourishing congregations believe that they must strategically take it upon themselves to help the newcomers learn the culture, beliefs, rituals, and customs of the local congregation. In this regard Catholic infrastructure, such as its schools or Right of Christian Initiation of Adults, provide examples of intentional ways to help socialize people into local congregational life.

Of course as individuals are drawn into the fellowship of a local congregation there are ways to deepen one's connection to other members. Leaders shared with us various ways that this occurred within their particular contexts, from small discussion or Bible study or prayer groups, to volunteer opportunities, to personal stories and testimonies that are shared in the weekly liturgy. One Roman Catholic priest in Ontario used the metaphor of family to describe hospitable community in his parish and the importance of participation, especially in the liturgy:

> Everybody in my eyes, the concept of a flourishing congregation would be everyone has a place in the family. Doesn't matter if there's thirty people or thirty thousand people, everyone has to have a place in that family ... in terms of liturgy, I think it's important that people feel part of the preparations. We have ministers of hospitality, we have people who read, we have a children's liturgy. And again I encourage everyone to become involved in the parish at some level.

What are the indicators that people feel connected to their congregation? As this priest suggested, it could be that members are actively engaged in their church community and that they feel a sense of pride in their congregation. He said: "A manifestation of a sense of belonging is their engagement in the community life, first, either through a formal ministry. Secondly, their frequent attendance that whenever they are here, you really see them and you can sense a sense of pride in them that they love this parish, that they really want to be counted as people who belong here."

From past research we know that as people feel a stronger sense of connection to the congregation, they are more likely to reciprocate with higher levels of involvement, volunteering, and financial contributions for the overall well-being of the congregation (Ammerman 2005; Bickers 2005; Bowen 2013; Bruce, Woolever, Wulff & Smith-Williams 2006; Carroll 2006; Dudley, Carroll & Wind 1991; Hopewell 1987; Reimer 2012;

Roozen & Hadaway 1993; Scheitle & Finke 2008; Wilkes 2001a, 2001b; Woolever & Bruce 2004).

Neighborhood Presence and Involvement

Neighbourhood Presence and Involvement
- "Incarnational presence" or "Being the hands and feet of Jesus"
- Community would notice if they left

AMBROSE
UNIVERSITY

As those we interviewed associated a hospitable community with a flourishing congregation, leaders, particularly Protestant ones, were adamant that this hospitality extended beyond the walls of the congregation. In their minds and experiences, flourishing congregations have an active presence and involvement in the welfare and justice of their neighborhood. Often framed in explicitly theological language such as "incarnational presence" or "being the hands and feet of Jesus," those we interviewed strongly resisted any notion that a flourishing congregation could exist solely for itself; congregations ought to be actively involved to better their communities, something that leaders of most congregations we interviewed believed was a reality in their contexts. One Maritime conservative Protestant pastor puts it this way:

> We run a program here in the community as well as downstairs for preschool children in the winter. So this area downstairs is the playground and it is open two or three mornings a week to preschool families. So, in terms of the community, the café, the ice cream and the indoor playground are a big community thing and we host community health programs here we well from the community health team. So, it is not exactly a community centre but there is a lot of coming and going.

Upon hearing stories such as this one, we often encountered participants who raised the question, "Would our community notice if we were no longer here?" This was frequently followed by an affirmative response.

There are several lines of inquiry that we would like to explore regarding congregational activities in their neighborhoods. What motivates congregations to be actively involved in their surrounding communities? Is this impulse primarily driven by theological commitments? Is there something about brand image at work where congregations seek to challenge negative Canadian perceptions toward organized religious groups by getting actively involved among those in the community who are skeptical or even hostile towards Christianity? Do people find their ways into active involvement in these congregations due to a particular congregation's involvement in their larger community? This last question is prompted by one congregation we visited. They go through the community and pick up and dispose of garbage that the city refuses. A lady showed up to that church and when asked if she knew someone at the church she said, "Oh no. I just figured any church that is willing to take care of my garbage is worth visiting." We wonder whether this narrative is the norm or the exception, or somewhere in-between.

Evangelism

Evangelism

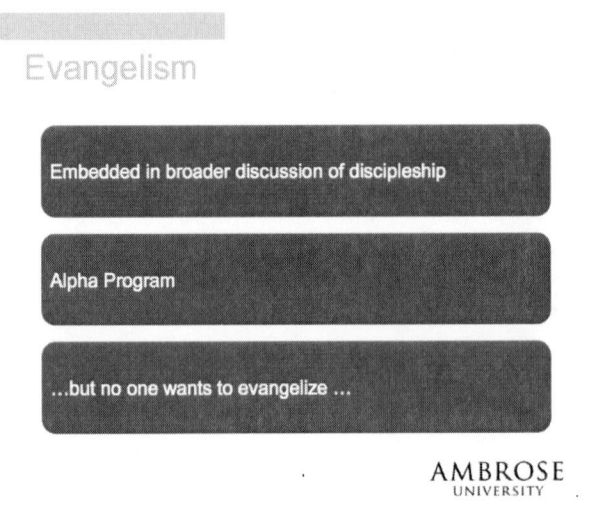

- Embedded in broader discussion of discipleship
- Alpha Program
- ...but no one wants to evangelize...

AMBROSE UNIVERSITY

Along with participating in "good works" in society, leaders across traditions and regions consistently singled out evangelism as an important marker of a flourishing congregation. One interviewee said:

> When I think of flourishing ... there is a real sense that people are coming to faith and are growing in their faith, and evangelistic communities have typically measured conversion and that's a really difficult thing to play with. And so we really look in terms of where baptism occurs and where it occurs in a discipleship journey, and does it lead to ongoing discipleship?

> Where there's baptism that leads to ongoing discipleship, people are flourishing and where that's happening lots of congregations are flourishing.

For those leaders who stressed quantitative aspects of flourishing, they did not mince words on the centrality of congregations who grew by way of new conversions. A denominational leader declared, "If you go to a church of 100 and you reach 10 people that's significant. And if you go to church of 1,000 and you reach 50 people, you should not be celebrating. You should be crying."

We were caught off guard to hear how many congregations in Catholic, mainline Protestant, and conservative Protestant settings had active evangelism focused programs – most notably the Alpha program, which was started with Nicky Gumbel in London, England. This program was designed to guide people who are invited to explore Christianity through a series of talks and discussions on core Christian beliefs and practices. The prevalence of an evangelistic focus, and the Alpha Program specifically, was surprising to us for two reasons. First, several traditions who, sometimes, are not associated with an evangelistic focus (e.g., Catholic and mainline Protestant) raved about how central and effective this program was to their congregation's activities. Second, given the general Canadian aversion to "pushy evangelism" (e.g., Adams 2006; Beyer & Ramji 2013; Reimer 2002; Thiessen 2015), we had not anticipated that Canadian congregations would indicate that they had taken up overt evangelism strategies. Those we interviewed did acknowledge the perceived Canadian aversion to evangelism in the form of verbal proclamation (which a number lamented, particularly in ethnic congregations and evangelical settings). A denominational leader, from a conservative Protestant context, said: "I would add

Evangelism as a separate point: Because that is the elephant in the room in Canada. Nobody likes it, nobody wants to do it, nobody wants anything to do with it."

What remains to be seen from phase one interviews and focus groups is how effective these evangelism initiatives were perceived to be. Are new people joining the Christian faith and local congregations in response to the Alpha program? Are flourishing congregations growing in large part due to conversion, and if so, what percentage of these congregations' growth might one attribute to conversion growth (in contrast to transfer growth, for example)? We have our doubts that congregations are growing mainly due to conversion, based on existing data regarding evangelical congregations in Canada (Reimer & Wilkinson 2015). Revelations from many leaders that the majority of their congregations were filled with those born and raised within their congregation or those who have transferred from another congregation has added to our suspicion about the effectiveness of evangelism. Few informants reported percentages higher than 5-10% of those who were converts resulting from evangelistic initiatives of one sort or another. But our anticipated phase three surveys directly working with congregants themselves should help us to test these ideas further; perhaps including a closer examination into the modes and mechanisms that evangelism is practiced and experienced in congregations across Christian traditions and Canadian regions.

Diversity

Diversity

DIVERSITY

Race, gender, social class, sexual orientation, and age

Effective conflict resolution skills

Questioning and uncertainty welcome

AMBROSE UNIVERSITY

A recurring refrain that we heard in focus groups and interviews was that flourishing congregations are diverse communities or ought to be. As we pressed participants about what exactly they had in mind, they mainly pointed toward any or all of the following: race, gender, social class, sexual orientation, and age. They also framed language about diversity in theological language about God's kingdom. During one focus group someone expressed:

> I think that if you don't have a fairly rich diversity within your church, it should reflect the demographic diversity of the community. If you don't have that diversity either social, economic diversity, or ethnic diversity, or both, I don't think you can actually say this is a flourishing congregation on biblical grounds. I think you can have a large congregation, but

if you don't have that diversity, I'm not sure you're reflecting the kingdom.

Another member of the group, a conservative Protestant pastor, stressed, "I think a flourishing congregation is one that's diverse in its generation, in its ethnicities. I think a comment was made in the focus group – it reflects the community it's in … If your church is all white and it's surrounded by tons of different ethnic populations, I wonder what's going on there. Like if there's an unawareness about that, that's really sad."

Recent research has revealed that ethnic diversity is more common in Canadian congregations than in the United States (see Bird 2015; Reimer & Wilkinson 2015). Ethnic diversity was a narrative that we heard loud and clear in all Catholic interviews, and to a lesser extent in some conservative Protestant settings. This narrative was also prominent in the major urban centers of Toronto, Vancouver, and Calgary, revealing the impact that contextual and demographic variables seemingly had on congregational life.

In addition to ethnic diversity, a leader in Winnipeg talked of the millionaire sitting alongside the unemployed in his congregation; while other leaders spoke of members of the LGBTQ community actively participating as full members in their congregation (especially in United Church of Canada and millennial-based congregations). Some leaders said that the various expressions of diversity discussed thus far was a lived reality from their leadership group through to those sitting in the pews; while for others they agreed that diversity is important but that diversity remained an aspiration that their congregations was pursuing.

Amidst the discussion about diversity, several leaders articulated their commitment to a congregational culture where questioning and uncertainty regarding one's faith was welcomed, and even preferred. A homogeneous congregation that stifles diverse questions, doubts, and experiences was stigmatized as a congregation that surely was not flourishing (even if its numeric metrics seem impressive). A United Church of Canada minister reflected:

> In our community, who would be flourishing, would be curiosity, openness, questions, non-prescriptive theology, more descriptive ... Our experience is that people are seeking belonging and then they want to figure out how it's worked and then they finally figure out what they believe. Which might be unique to our community, but it's certainly thriving because people are welcome to question and they come aware that that's biblical and essential to a flourishing faith. That may not be perceived by others as the right way but certainly our community is a seeking kind of community. So the thriving to me or flourishing is: there's a certain element of doubt that is curiosity that is like Thomas, and is willing to question.

A denominational leader in the Anglican Church of Canada put it this way:

> To be transparent and have candor and even in the midst of disagreements to not have that kind of nicey-nice and suck it up and stew later. But we can put it on the table because we're adults and healthy and we can have a conversation even if we disagree. And we don't have to leave the table and no one's asking anyone to leave the table. And I think that's key to a flourishing congregation in terms of those conversations. Are

we able to have healthy holy conversations and that kind of thing?

With diversity and the openness to people openly and honestly grappling with their uncertainties in community, conflict was inevitable. We gathered from many of our conversations that flourishing congregations were characterized by strong conflict resolution skills. By this we understood that interviewed leaders believed that to effectively help their congregation to navigate conflict they need to do so skillfully and in theologically sound ways (which we assume means different things to members of different theological traditions). Below are two lengthier reflections, the first from a denominational leader in the Anglican Church of Canada, and the second from a local United Church of Canada minister.

> When conflict arises because inevitably it will, the congregation can handle it, can deal with it a respectful and mature manner. Does not devolve into horrible cliques or factions. Does not try to kill the leadership or kill the messenger for the presence of the problem. Can see the conflict as an opportunity for clarifying self-identity, increasing commitment in leadership, increasing growth and orienting towards the future, etcetera, etcetera; can actually see the things that arise in community life which we inevitably do as opportunities rather than threats … if internally you've got a congregation that is terrified of conflict and terrified of failure and terrified of risk, terrified of taking creative risks and possibly messing something up, then these will be superficial signs. If I think about the flourishing congregations that I carry in my head and the stories I'm carrying in my head right now, they have all done something good in relation to conflict

… They've just relaxed about conflict. They just have relaxed and said, 'You know, sometimes we're going to have to ask people to change seats on the bus,' so leadership issues. And sometimes they'll get pissed off and leave the bus and that's okay. I think of the moment in this congregation that – two moments in this congregation where we really started to grow and flourish a little bit in numbers but more so in maturity and dynamism was when we spoke frankly about some real conflict at the ending of the previous staff configuration team. We dropped into talking circles with real sharing of pain, different points of view, but listening with respect. And then that was replicated when we did a year and a half process moving towards same sex marriage. And there was a disagreement in the congregation and the congregation had been split over the ordination of gays and lesbians. So there was that. It was like a bomb planted underground, you know? And it wasn't so much diffusing the bomb as a controlled explosion of it so that the energy came out that could be managed and actually turned into energy for the life of the community. I think one of the things that is characteristic of so many of our not flourishing congregations is we're frozen by the fear of the conflict. And we have a deep intuition that we ain't getting from where we are to where we want to be without some people getting ticked off and maybe leaving. And finding a way into thawing that frozenness and living with courage and confidence is really very liberating.

As our project unfolds, we have several questions that we want to explore regarding diversity. Are flourishing congregations actually diverse, and if so, along what social lines? Do members of different subgroups interact with members of other subgroups in a congregation, and if so, in what context and manner do they do so? How do members feel and act toward people of "other" groups in the congregation, however defined? How are diverse perspectives among and between church leaders and congregants presented and approached in settings where leaders value questioning and uncertainty?

Discussion and Conclusion

Discussion and Conclusion

- Aware of highly secular context in Canada – contributes to a sense of urgency and action
- Alert to negative perceptions toward Christianity and congregations – striving to repair "brand image"
- Diversity

AMBROSE
UNIVERSITY

Three conclusions stand out from this early sampling of our exploratory research into flourishing congregations in Canada. First, Canadian church leaders are keenly aware of the secular context that they find themselves in. In this environment congregations struggle to attract and retain members. In the minds of some, Christianity is moving further to the margins of Canadian social life. This narrative figured prominently for leaders of flourishing congregations who had honed their congregations' identities to respond to and engage this cultural milieu. These are leaders who claimed to equip and empower other leaders with an eye toward the future of their congregation in a sea of congregations that were fighting for survival. Congregations who took risks and tried new things, from evangelism initiatives to open conversations as part of weekly liturgies, were aware that the status quo would not suffice for them; and these congregations demarcated clear structures and processes to help people join and get involved in congregational life. Overall, these leaders perceived that Canadian congregations were desperate in an increasingly secular context and they acted accordingly to pursue a state of thriving rather than merely surviving.

Second, interview and focus group participants seemed acutely conscious of the prevailing negative images that many Canadians have toward Christians and congregations. We wonder whether this awareness has served as a part of the motivation for leaders of flourishing congregations to intentionally strengthen and improve their image with current and possible members. Flattening the hierarchy in some ways and fostering shared ownership over a congregation's identity and activities among congregants are some of the ways that flourishing congregations accomplish this. So, too, are shifts to include more space for dialogue and conversation in weekly congregational gatherings. Active involvement in neighborhoods, using the Alpha Program to engage those outside of Christianity, and forming hospitable communities for newcomers, in particular, were all evident in perceptions expressed by leaders as they thought of flourishing congregations. Collectively, denominational and local pastors knew that flourishing congregations in Canada were experiencing a "brand" problem and they were intentionally pursuing strategies to gradually change people's perceptions and experiences in and through their congregations.

Third, lived experiences and aspirations of diversity is interesting to note. Of course, Canada has a longstanding value for diversity and tolerance in its many forms, and leaders of congregations who we spoke with evidently do as well. Leaders connected to selected Canadian congregations in this research saw diversity as a hallmark of a flourishing congregation. This could reveal the influences of Canadian culture, various theological frameworks, or both. It seems that there is something at work here that possibly sets Canadian congregational understandings apart from those in the United States.

We do not claim that each of the findings discussed are new. These findings and insights do confirm some of what we already know from the literature. This study is different in that it moves us toward a better understanding of flourishing congregations in a distinctly Canadian context, as identified and experienced from Canadian church leaders across the Christian spectrum. How and why do congregations flourish in Canada when the general story of religious decline pervades? This study begins a process to investigate and identify the narratives, processes, contexts, and legitimation structures of flourishing congregations in a pervasively secular Canadian environment.

Looking Forward

As we continue to analyze our data and begin to disseminate our findings from phase one interviews and focus groups, we look ahead to phase two research wherein we propose to invite nine congregational case studies in Calgary, Alberta with three Catholic, three mainline Protestant (Anglican, United Church of Canada, Presbyterian), and three conservative Protestant (Christian and Missionary Alliance, Baptist, Evangelical Covenant) congregations to work with us. Our central question in phase two will be: what are the social narratives, experiences, processes, conditions, and theological reasons that contribute to people joining and getting involved in flourishing congregations – Catholic, mainline, and conservative Protestant – in Canada?

In phase three we have planned a national survey with 1500+ who attend flourishing congregations across Canada. Our central aim in this survey will be to test a number of the questions and hypotheses raised in this paper, as well as new questions to emerge in our current data analysis from phase one plus the findings from phase two. We anticipate that this survey will give us a window into some of the demographic realities and perspectives among congregants themselves that may validate or challenge some of what we have heard from leaders in phase one of the project.

Section IV

flourishing
CONGREGATIONS
INSTITUTE

Closing Engagement & Remarks

In the context of the Flourishing Congregations Institute launch, we invited Dr. Reginald Bibby (University of Lethbridge) and Dr. Sam Reimer (Crandall University) to join in a conversation about the two papers (above) and their general thoughts on the themes raised. Their session and the presentation of the two papers are available on the following URL:
http://www.flourishingcongregations.org/resources

We then asked Sam Reimer to share a few comments with us. We also invited Dr. Linda Schwartz, Dean of Arts and Science at Ambrose University, and Dr. Jo-Ann Badley, Dean of Theology at Ambrose University and Seminary, to offer a reflection on the possible benefits of this research Institute for Ambrose.

Closing Engagement

Dr. Sam Reimer, Professor of Sociology, Crandall University

Dr. Reimer commented on the privilege it was to be with Dr. Reg Bibby. He said that he had read *Fragmented Gods* in 1988. Without Dr. Bibby's excellent work on religion in Canada over three decades, we would know much less about religion in Canada. Sam Reimer then made the following remarks and responses to four questions:

- a. Its time we had a flourishing congregations study in Canada, and it might be that we haven't until now because
  - Most people thought that religion was on its way out so there would not be any flourishing congregations by now
  - Because the idea of flourishing congregations in not very Canadian. Sounds more like the US when bigger, successful, and competitive is better.
- b. Good to allow for movement in definition, but reality requires characteristics to start. Good list given, and I think best work here is from NCLS in Australia that gives 9 qualities of vital congregations based on their research.

1. **What are we hearing?**
   - Themes re: context in Canada Not about the numbers
   - Clear self-identity
   - Spiritual experience and transformed lives
   - Discipleship

- Leadership (strategic and collaborative,, spirit led, supported pastor)
- Think outside the box (take risks, learn from failures)
- Hospitable community (plan for integrating members, sense of belonging)
- Neighborhood outreach (missional, would they notice if we are gone)
- Evangelism
- Diversity

a. **Clarity about the secular context**- how do we thrive in a secular milieu? Negative image of Christian congregations. Probably a **growing minority antagonistic** to Christianity. There still seems to be a large ambivalent middle in Canada that sees both pros and cons to religion. These are people that are open to religious involvement, (as Bibby has noted) but aren't dropping in (and are unlikely to do so as Thiessen has noted). Now, they are increasingly likely to say that they are "nones" than before. I wonder if the negativity some perceive toward religion is less of a "I was hurt by or I dislike religion" and more of a **handy justification** for their lack of participation. I wonder if this is also why so many Canadians seem interested in stories of moral failure of religious leaders and injustices by religious organizations.

b. **Comparisons with religion elsewhere**

- **Diversity** is good in and of itself- **difference from US?** Yes in terms of scope and clearly among the less active and educated evangelicals. But when I talked to MP and even EP in the US they were all over diversity, and the Eps were all over racial diversity, esp the Pentecostals.

2. **What would be useful to analyze initial findings.**
    - I wish I did more in my book, good case of do as I say, not as I do.
    - Need to start with **characteristics and narratives**, but then the hard work comes.
    a. **Identifying underlying mechanisms** – I would say that another list of characteristics of flourishing congregations is useful (partly because of the Canadian context) but more useful would be discovering the mechanisms which account for the presence/absence of these characteristics. This is not quite like independent variables, which tend to be demographics (like age, ethnic diversity, education) that are correlated with a positive characteristic, say community outreach. These independent variables only lead to where to look for these mechanisms. Say that I find a congregations that are a strong outreach program tend to have a more educated laity. This is interesting, and may even be a necessary but not sufficient condition. More interesting is isolating those mechanisms that activate educated laity to reach out. Is it something in the environment, like the presentation of a clear need that triggers it? Or maybe a deep personal spirituality in the educated laity? Or both? I would say that key to your research is uncovering and isolating those mechanisms that allow dormant potentialities to be activated.
    - An example: the denominational leaders I have talked to about vital congregations say that the key ingredient

is **strong leadership** in a congregation. Naturally, denominational leaders focus on internal factors and emphasize those that they relate to. No doubt leadership is key, because we know that motivation, articulation of clear vision owned by all, strategic planning and measurement of outcomes are all key. But sociologists tell us that **external factors** are more important than internal factors, factors like a growing neighborhood around the church, a lack of similar congregations in close proximity, and the sort. Who is right? Well, it is probably both. Good leadership helps identify potentialities and mobilize congregants toward outreach into the neighborhood, which ultimately draws people who are lapsed affiliates, or seekers from the neighborhood. That is, **the growing neighborhood that contains potential affiliates is necessary condition for growth, but the mechanism of good leadership activates that potentiality.**

- Many of these mechanisms cannot be measured, but can only be theorized. What you measure often tells you where to look. Then it is up to you researchers to identify the most plausible explanation for the interesting confluence of different factors, and then test your theory to see if it resonates with religious leaders.

b. **What is measured becomes prescriptive**- I think one of the unintended consequences of studying congregations is that what is measured becomes prescriptive. That is, what social scientists intend to be descriptive becomes prescriptive because that is what

we talk about. Hard measures of flourishing like increased weekly attendance became a prescriptive partly because, since McGarvan and the church growth movement, that was something that was easy to measure. And since research presents data on numerical growth so much, it becomes the default way of understanding vitality. And church leaders start counting butts in the pews and feeling good or bad about what they are doing based on whether that number is up or down. In other words. Its like telling our children who watch 10s of thousands of TV advertisements that they buying things won't make you happy.
- A hazard of being a researcher is that we are actually being prescriptive when we intend only to be My point is that one of our hazards descriptive.

c. Problem with soft and hard measures
- Recently I was asked to measure missional church priorities. I discovered that was nearly impossible. How do you quantify incarnational outreach or inner transformation besides asking very soft measures, like "Do you feel you are engaged in incarnational outreach?" never mind the confusion out there about what missional church actually means. Or, do you think that you are being personally transformed? Are there any objective measures of this? We can ask people how many hours a week they volunteer in the community, but this is again fraught with all sorts of problems of memory and desireability bias.

3. **Research on congregations should have on their radar**
   - Evangelical congregations are no longer growing, so I think they need to do
   - **Cooperation** is more the norm in Canada as denominationalism is less important. It seems like mainline Protestants cooperate across faiths, whereas my evidence suggests that that is rare for evangelicals, who cooperate with EP, MP and Cath.
   - **Immigration** impact on Christianity is hard to underestimate. About 70% of population growth in Canada is accounted for by immigration, and about 90% in 2050. Fertility is low (1.6) and conversions are few. Still, almost ½ of new immigrants (47% between 2006-11) are Christian, and they are more likely to be EP, then Cath, then MP. Most of the growth in our churches/denominations is from immigration. So how we welcome and integrate them is important.
   - **Large churches** - there are few in Canada, even proportionally. 2.3% of prot churches in US are 1000+ and 0.8% in Canada. Why? Smaller more spread out population, lower church attendance, smaller proportion of evangelicals (71% of large churches are evangelical in US), less entrepreneurial spirit/leaders, and maybe some anti-American sentiment.
4. **What practical insights for church and denominational leaders**
   - **View of evangelicals** - With Trump's election and his support from evangelicals, the tendency to paint EP in Canada with a US brush will likely increase, and will negative attitudes toward EPs.

- **Canada looking like England**- If this is correct, then Grace Davie's idea of "vicarious religion" in England is interesting. She claims that Christianity is expected to be tarry to marry and bury. They are to be religious vicariously for others, and are expected to say things like "marriage is sacred and it to last until death due us part" regardless of what those involved actually believe. Could make refusals to marry or bury less acceptable.
- **Move from external to internal locus of authority**
- **Plant churches**

Closing Remarks

Dr. Linda Schwartz

Dean of Arts and Science, Ambrose University

No flourishing congregation exists without a dynamic and committed laity. In church life, vocation and service come together, and the gathered community, in turn, provides a spiritual home, energizing and equipping people of faith from all walks of life to do what they do every working day. The Faculty of Arts and Science at Ambrose University aims to equip graduates in the humanities, social sciences, business, education and the fine arts to be seekers after truth and to be redemptively engaged with the culture. At Ambrose, the faculty is committed to formation that encourages students to engage redemptively, as Christ followers, at every intersection or opportunity where faith can speak into public discourses and issues or questions of ethical, societal and cultural import.

This new Institute is a significant development in Ambrose's intention to **inform** our students about the religious and cultural landscape which they inhabit, to **underline** the importance with which their own contribution - in the church and in society - needs to be thoughtful, vital, relevant, and oriented toward redemptive engagement in their world and community contexts, and to **encourage** them by a modelling a relational stance toward self-actualization as people of faith who **both depend on** and **draw** from vital experiences within a relevant covenanting community and who go from this place to be theologically reflective agents of transformation in their several vocations.

I want to thank my colleagues for their passionate investment in this project. It models for our students in Arts and Science programs, and indeed our entire community at Ambrose, that deep commitment to understanding a transformative vision of the **church** as localized, particular and flourishing. Our students need to know three things that your work is uncovering about flourishing congregations:

1. That a flourishing congregation is a locus of both **invocation and vocation**;
2. That flourishing communities hold to a confessing witness that ordains all people of faith to exercise a shared **call and responsibility to be the body of Christ in the world,** through the **incarnational** celebration of the sacraments (which is one of the marks of a 'flourishing' community);
3. That to flourish is to orient or reorient toward the notion of the worshipping community as the sacred space where gifts of the laity are discerned, affirmed, developed, and offered for service, empowered by a transforming vision that is only possible through the guidance of the Holy Spirit.

In this capacity, the flourishing congregation and the Christian university share a common task of discipleship formation that prepares our graduates for lives of positive, thoughtful and transformative engagement and influence, as agents of grace that are the hands, feet, eyes, ears and voice of our Lord in their communities, our nation and the world. (Please permit an observation: if our students - some of whom experience intensive and intentional manifestations of faith community at Ambrose - cannot find welcoming communities that have a passion to 'seek justice and love mercy', they will create alternative spaces and places to worship and serve - and flourish.)

Thank you, colleagues, for this gift of your time and scholarly capacity, to us at Ambrose. We hope this gift will be as meaningful to us in realizing our university mission as it is to those many denominational groups who have chosen to engage with this longitudinal and phased study and reflection.

Closing Remarks

Dr. Jo-Ann Badley

Dean of Theology, Ambrose University and Seminary

Theology is the study of God. But the study of God is not like the study of biology, where you have bugs or plants or whatever that you can focus on. Rather we are studying what we cannot see, and must be satisfied with studying the traces of God's presence, whether in scripture, or history, or current society. Or reflecting on a synthesis of such traces, such as we do in theology proper.

And so sociological work, describing the church in Canada, such as this team is doing, is very important. And I am grateful that they are doing this work.

But it points to the ways such work has to be put into conversation with other work, and this is an interdisciplinary conversation that I am looking forward to. This conversation has been called for today by those who remember previous (Canadian church) initiatives that didn't work, or with scripture stories that speak of another kind of experience (Acts).

And it also reminds us to be careful about the categories we use in the work—and here my hope is that this work will move from general categories to more specific ones that need to inform our work: rural churches, ethnic churches, new church initiatives, mega churches. Which the team has indicated is its intent.

And as my colleague Terry Young reminds me, as much as we might wish for a silver bullet, there isn't one. That this conversation may give general indications of the direction of the church in society, but that specific church situations will be influenced by factors that no one has taken into account.

Editors' Postscript

As we intimated in our preface, much of the script is yet to be written for the Flourishing Congregations Institute. The conversations we had and the feedback we received during and after our launch have been immensely helpful during these formative stages of the Institute. We are encouraged with our general trajectory, yet mindful that we have much to think about and act on. This is only the beginning.

Already we have discerned that our second phase of research ought to pivot toward a national survey where we tease out what we think we are hearing from phase one interviews and focus groups. Doing so will allow us to construct and assess our emerging conception of the characteristics and traits associated with a flourishing congregation in Canada, and importantly to compare these findings along several variables (e.g. leaders and congregants, theological tradition, church size, rural and urban locations, regions across Canada, etc.). Should all of the pieces come together for this endeavour, we anticipate launching a national survey in Fall 2017, with early dissemination of results sometime in Spring 2018. And perhaps in-depth case studies will follow this survey.

Looking ahead we plan to have many more conversations, to strengthen existing and forge new partnerships, and to listen carefully to the wisdom and insight of Canadian scholars and church leaders across the theological spectrum. We do so with a posture of humility, eager to learn and contribute positively to the Church in Canada.

Selected References

Adams, Michael. 2006. *Sex in the Snow: The Surprising Revolution in Canadian Social Values*. Toronto: Penguin.

Ammerman, Nancy T. 1997. *Congregation and Community*. New Brunswick, NJ: Rutgers University Press.

------. 2005. *Pillars of Faith: American Congregations and their Partners*. Berkeley, CA: University of California Press.

Ammerman, Nancy T., Jackson W. Carroll, Carl S. Dudley and William McKinney, eds. 1998. *Studying Congregations: A New Handbook*. Nashville, TN: Abingdon Press.

Angus Reid Institute. 2015. "Religion and Faith in Canada Today: Strong Belief, Ambivalence, and Rejection Define Our Views." Retrieved 27 March 2015 (http://angusreid.org/wp-content/uploads/2016/01/2015.03.25_Faith.pdf).

Beyer, Peter, and Rubina Ramji, eds. 2013. *Growing Up Canadian: Muslims, Hindus, Buddhists*. Montreal: McGill-Queen's University Press.

Bibby, Reginald. 2011. *Beyond the Gods and Back: Religion's Demise and Rise and Why it Matters*. Lethbridge, AB: Project Canada Books.

Bibby, Reginald and Angus Reid. 2016. *Canada's Catholics: Vitality and Hope in a New Era*. Toronto, ON: Novalis.

Bickers, Dennis W. 2005. *The Healthy Small Church*. Kansas City: Beacon Hill Press.

Bird, Warren. 2015. "Large Canadian Churches Drawn an Estimated 300,000 Worshippers Each Week: Findings From a National Study." Retrieved 27 October 2015 (http://leadnet.org/canada/).

Bowen, John, ed. 2013. *Green Shoots out of Dry Ground: Growing a New Future for the Church in Canada*. Eugene, OR: Wipf and Stock.

Bramadat, Paul, and David Seljak, eds. 2008. *Christianity and Ethnicity in Canada*. Toronto, ON: University of Toronto Press.

Bruce, D., C. Woolever, K. Wulff and I. Smith-Williams. 2006. "Fast-growing churches: What Distinguishes Them From Others?" *Journal of Beliefs & Values* 27 (1): 111-126.

Carroll, Jackson W. 2006. *God's Potters: Pastoral Leadership and the Shaping of Congregations*. Grand Rapids, MI: Eerdmans.

Chaves, Mark and Shawna L. Anderson. 2014. "Changing American Congregations: Findings from the Third Wave of the National Congregations Study." *Journal for the Scientific Study of Religion* 53 (4): 676-86.

Dudley, Carl S. and Sally A. Johnson. 1993. *Energizing the Congregation: Images that Shape Your Church's Ministry*. Louisville, KY: Westminster/John Knox Press.

Dudley, Carl, Jackson W. Carroll and James P. Wind, eds. 1991. *Carriers of Faith: Lessons from Congregational Studies.* Louisville, KY: Westminster/John Knox Press.

Fleenor, J. W. 2006. *Trait Approach to Leadership. Encyclopedia of Industrial and Organizational Psychology.* New York, NY: SAGE Publications.

Haskell, David, Kevin Flatt and Stephanie Burgoyne. 2016. "Theology Matters: Comparing the Traits of Growing and Declining Mainline Protestant Church Attendees and Clergy." *Review of Religious Research* 58 (4): 515-541.

Hersey, P., K. Blanchard and D. Johnson 2012. *Management of Organizational Behaviors: Leading Human Resources. 10th Edition.* Upper Saddle River, NJ: Pearson Prentice Hall.

Hoge, Dean A. and David A. Roozen, eds. 1979. *Understanding Church Growth and Decline: 1950-1978.* New York, NY: The Pilgrim Press.

Holling, C.S. 2001. "Understanding the Complexity of Economic, Ecological, and Social Systems." *Ecosystems* 4: 390-405.

Hopewell, James F. 1987. *Congregation: Stories and Structures.* Philadelphia, PA: Fortress Press.

House, R.J. 1996. "Path-goal Theory of Leadership: Lessons, Legacy, and a Reformulated Theory. *Leadership Quarterly* 7 (3): 323–52.

Marti, Gerardo and Gladys Ganiel. 2014. *The Deconstructed Church: Understanding Emerging Christianity.* New York, NY. Oxford University Press.

McMullin, Steve. 2013. "The Secularization of Sunday: Real or Perceived Competition for Churches." *Review of Religious Research* 55 (1): 43-59.

McGavran, Donald A. 1990. *Understanding Church Growth.* 3rd edition (revised and edited by C. Peter Wagner). Grand Rapids, MI: Eerdmans.

Noll, Mark. 1992. *A History of Christianity in the United States and Canada.* Grand Rapids, MI: William B. Eerdmans Publishing Company.

Parson, George and Speed B. Leas. 1993. *Understanding Your Congregation as a System.* Washington, DC: Alban Institute.

Reimer, Sam. 2003. *Evangelicals and the Continental Divide: The Conservative Protestant Subculture in Canada and the United States.* Montreal: McGill-Queen's University Press.

------. 2012. "Congregational Vitality among Evangelical Churches in Canada." *Church and Faith Trends* 5 (1): 1-17.

Reimer, Sam and Michael Wilkinson. 2015. *A Culture of Faith: Evangelical Congregations in Canada.* Montreal, QC: McGill-Queen's University Press.

Roozen, David and C. Kirk Hadaway, eds. 1993. *Church and Denominational Growth: What Does (and Does not) Cause Growth or Decline*. Nashville, TN: Abingdon Press.

Saarinen, Martin F. 1986. *The Life Cycle of a Congregation*. Washington, DC: Alban Institute.

Scazzero, Peter. 2010. *The Emotionally Healthier Church*. Grand Rapids, MI: Zondervan.

Scheitle, Christopher P. and Kevin D. Dougherty. 2008. "The Sociology of Religious Organizations." *Sociology Compass* 2/3: 981-999.

Scheitle, Christopher P. and Roger Finke. 2008. "Maximizing Congregational Resources: Selection versus Production." *Social Science Research* 37: 815-827.

Schwarz, Christian A. 1998. *Natural Church Development: A Guide to Eight Essential Qualities of Healthy Churches*. 3rd edition. Carol Stream, IL: ChurchSmart Resources.

Stark, Rodney and Roger Finke. 2000. *Acts of Faith: Explaining the Human Side of Religion*. Berkeley, CA: University of California Press.

Stark, Rodney, and William Sims Bainbridge. 1985. *The Future of Religion: Secularization, Revival, and Cult Formation*. Berkeley: University of California Press.

Statistics Canada. 2013. "Immigration and Ethnocultural Diversity in Canada." Retrieved 20 May 2013 (http://www12.statcan.gc.ca/nhs-enm/2011/as-sa/99-010-x/99-010-x2011001-eng.pdf).

Thiessen, Joel. 2015. *The Meaning of Sunday: The Practice of Belief in a Secular Age*. Montreal, QC: McGill-Queen's University Press.

Wagner, Peter C. 1976. *Your Church Can Grow*. Glendale, CA: G/L Publications.

Weber, Max. 1949. *The Methodology of the Social Sciences*. Glencoe, IL: Free Press.

Wilkes, Paul. 2001a. *Excellent Catholic Parishes: The Guide to Best Places and Practices*. New York, NY: Paulist Press.

Wilkes, Paul. 2001b. *Excellent Protestant Congregations: The Guide to Best Places and Practices*. Louisville, KY: Westminister/John Knox Press.

Wilkins-Laflamme, Sarah. 2014. "Towards Religious Polarization? Time Effects on Religious Commitment in US, UK and Canadian Regions." *Sociology of Religion* 75 (2): 284-308.

Wind, James P. and James W. Lewis, eds. 1994. *American Congregations: New Perspectives in the Study of Congregations. Volume 2*. Chicago, IL: The University of Chicago Press.

Woolever, Cynthia and Deborah Bruce. 2004. *Beyond the Ordinary: Ten Strengths of US Congregations*. Louisville, KY: Westminister/John Knox Press.

A Preliminary Look at Flourishing Congregations in Canada: What Church Leaders are Saying

Edited by Joel Thiessen, Arch Wong, Bill McAlpine, and Keith Walker

2017

Published by

Turning Point GLOBAL

A Free PDF version and information about how to obtain additional hardcopies of this monograph are found on Flourishing Congregation Institute Website: http://flourishingcongregations.org/